THE CRIMEA

A SHORT HISTORY

Also by M Clement Hall

Non-Fiction

The Locomotor System—Functional Anatomy
The Locomotor System—Functional Histology
Architecture of Bone; Luschka's Joint; Lessons in Histology
Palestine—The Price of Freedom; Intifada
IME—The Word Book; Independent Medical Examinations
The Fibromyalgia Controversy; Modern Eye Surgery; Aesthetic Surgery; Diabetes Mellitus
Washing Away of Wrongs; A Calendar of Miseries; Murder of Richard Hunne
Pope Innocent III; Saint Benedict of Nursia
The Canadian Health System; My Surgery – My Surgeon

Charles River e-books

Arab Spring; History of Afghanistan; History of Syria;
History of Ancient Egypt; History of Modern Egypt; History of Iran;
History of Hamas; History of Hezbollah
History of Charlemagne

Memoir

Viet Nam 1963; Viet Nam 1964-1966; Vale Viet Nam

Fiction

Trauma Surgeon; Spare Parts Box
The King George Inn; Diamonds in West Africa; Farmer George
Martin's Absolution; Martin in Byzantium

THE CRIMEA

A SHORT HISTORY

M Clement Hall

THE CRIMEA A SHORT HISTORY

Copyright © 2014 by M. Clement Hall

All rights reserved.

No part of this publication may be reproduced, stored in a retrieval system, or transmitted in any form or by any means, digital, electronic, mechanical, photocopying, recording, or otherwise, or conveyed via the Internet or a Web site without prior written permission of the author, except in the case of brief quotations embodied in critical articles and reviews.

ISBN: 978-1-304-97576-8

A VERY BRIEF ACCOUNT

OF THE VERY LONG

HISTORY OF THE CRIMEA

Crimea, or the Crimean Peninsula, located on the northern coast of the Black Sea, has a history of over 2000 years. The territory has been conquered and controlled many times throughout this history.

THE NAME

The name "Crimea" takes its origin in the name of the city of Qırım (today called Stary Krym) which served as a capital of the Crimean province of the Golden Horde. The ancient Greeks called Crimea Tauris (later Taurica), after its inhabitants, the Tauri.

Taurica was eventually renamed Golden Orde by the Crimean Tatars, from whose language the Crimea's modern name derives. The word "Crimea" comes from the Crimean Tatar name Qırım via Golden Orde Mongolia Kherem, Kerm (Wall or Fortress) or via Greek Krimeía (Κριμαία).

Since 1921, the name Taurida has had no official status in Crimea and is used almost only in historical context. However, some institutions of the republic still use it, for example Taurida National University, the main university in Crimea.

FC Tavriya Simferopol, a football club in Simferopol, adopted the name upon the collapse of the Soviet Union, when it became one of the top Ukrainian clubs.

THE LAND

It covers about 10,400 square miles, or approximately 27,000 square kilometers (for comparison Belgium is 30,278 square kms). At its widest point, from Saki to Kertch, at the eastern most tip of the Kertch Peninsula, it is about 150 miles, or 250 kilometers wide. It is about 100 miles, or 150 kilometers from the northernmost city of Perekop, which lies on the isthmus which connects Crimea to the mainland, to the southern tip near Yalta. The isthmus that joins the Crimea to the mainland is a mere 5 miles, or 8 km, wide. At one time, unknown inhabitants had attempted to build a canal across this isthmus, thus making the Crimea an island. The attempt failed, however, and the Crimea remains a peninsula.

The northern part of the Crimea consists of low steppes which cover three quarters of the Crimea, and the land gradually rises in the south to the Crimean mountains that hug the coast from Yalta to Feodosiya. The mountains drop steeply into the Black Sea, and shield the narrow coast lands from the wind. The climate here is subtropical. The grassy plains of the north furnish pasture for sheep and horse, and grains are grown on the flat steppes. The climate on the steppes is quite different, and winters are severe due to the cold Arctic winds that blow across the steppes from the north. In the south, where the climate is much more mild, grapes are grown in vineyards that dot the mountainsides. Salt is dried along the coasts, as the Black Sea is a salt water body. Resorts and health centers dot the the coasts, especially in the area from Yalta to Feodosiya, and here you can find the summer palaces of the Tsars.

The highest point of the Crimea is Roman-Kosh, 5,000 feet. The Crimean Mountains are divided into three ridges that run for 180 km from Sevestaspol to Feodosia. Along the South Ridge there is a narrow valley on the south side of the mountains, between the mountains and the sea. In present day Crimea, a canal which is 402 km long, provides water to the peninsula's towns and grain fields. This North Crimea Canal flows from north to south across the steppes.

The distance from Simferopol to Yalta is 96 km, and the distance can be spanned in modern day Crimea by what is the longest and highest trolley bus road in Europe. The capitol of Crimea is Simferopol, and other large cities include Sevastopol, Yevpatoria, Feodosia, Yalta, Kerch, Sudak, and the once famous capitol of the Khans,

Bahchisaray. Yalta is the region's most famous health resort. Sevestopol is an important naval base and was the site of the Crimean War conflict in 1854-1856.

BRIEF OVERVIEW OF HISTORY

The history of the Crimea is long and varied. It was first settled in the Early Paleolithic by the Cimmerians who lived on the peninsula in 15-7 BC. The coastal and mountainous regions were inhabited by the Taurians, after whom the peninsula was named Taurica.

In 4 BC, the Scythian kingdom was established on the Steppes of the Crimea. The Greeks also formed colonies nearby. The colony of Chersonese was established in the district of present day Sevastopol. At the beginning of the new era, the Scythian kingdom was conquered by the Germanic tribes of the Goths.

In the 4th century, the Crimea was invaded by the Huns who destroyed the greater part of the peninsula's population. Later the Khazar tribes, whose descendants are the Karaims, appeared on the land. They were first ousted by the Pechenegs, and later, by the Polovtsians.

The Slavs gained a foothold in the Crimea in the 10th century, and established the principality of Tmutorokan.

In the 13th century, some of the coastal lands were captured by Italian traders, partly controlled by the Venetians and partly by the Genovese.

During this century, Taurica was captured by the Mongols who gave the Crimea it's present day name of Kyrym (Krym). For two centuries, the Crimea was the seat of the Golden Horde and the Crimea became one of the largest slave trade markets.

In 1441, the Crimean Khanate was established by Haci Giray Khan, a direct descendent of Ghengis Khan. The Giray dynasty ruled Crimea without interruption until April 8, 1873 ; they were followed by the Crimean Khanate and the Ottoman Empire in the 15th to 18th centuries,

After winning a decisive victory in the Russo-Turkish War of 1768-1774, Russia annexed the Crimea under the rule of Catherine II. Due to the oppressive tsarist policy towards the Crimean Tatars, hundreds of thousands of Crimean Tatars left the Crimea in waves of massive migrations, which continued throughout Russia's rule of the Crimea.. The Crimean Tatar population was estimated to be over 5 million during the height of the Khanate rule, and decreased to less than 300,000 at the time of the Bolshevik Revolution.

After the annexation of the Crimea by Catherine II, the peninsula became the home to Ukrainians, Russians, Bulgarians, Germans, and Swiss. Many of the deserted Tatar villages were inhabited by these peoples who migrated into the Crimea at the invitation of Catherine II, but the Tatar village names were retained at the insistence of the Russian government. Villages also sprung up on the now vacant estates of the once bourgeois Tatars, and in many of these cases, the villages were named after the previous Tatar estate owners. Many German villages in the Crimea bear two names, one Tatar, one German, for example, one village is Byten (or Bjuten), which is the Tatar village name, and is also called Herrenhilf, which is the German village name.

There followed the Russian Empire in the 18th to 20th centuries, the Russian Soviet Federative Socialist Republic and later the Ukrainian Soviet Socialist Republic within the Soviet Union. In 1991 it became part of independent Ukraine, as the Autonomous Republic Crimea.

EARLY HISTORY

Taurica

The "Chersonesus Taurica" of Antiquity, shown on a map printed in London, ca 1770

Detail of map above

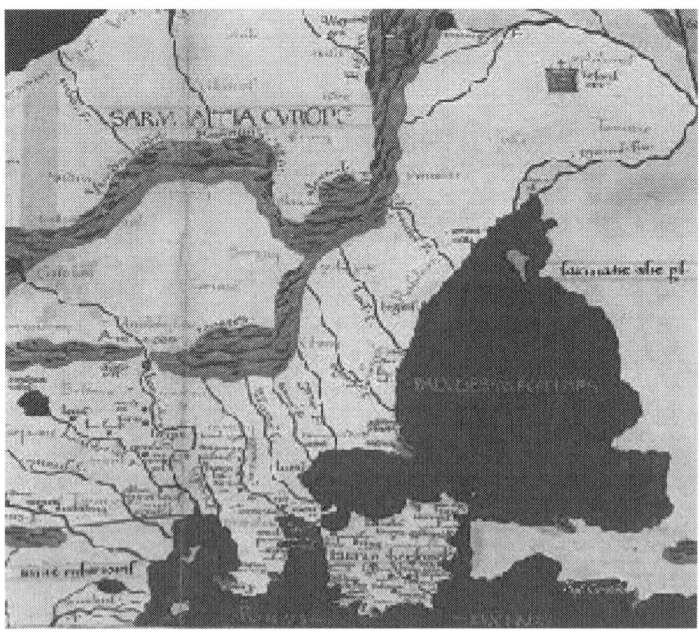

Ptolemy's Map

Taurica, Tauric Chersonese, and Tauris were names by which the territory of the Crimean Peninsula was known to the Greeks and Romans.

Etymology of the name

The Greeks named the region after its inhabitants, the Tauri. Chersonesus Taurica is the Latin version of the Greek name (*chersonese* means *peninsula*). This Latin variant of the name should not be confused with the city of Chersonesus in Taurica.

As the Tauri inhabited only mountainous regions of southern Crimea, at first the name was used only for this southern part, but later it was extended to the whole peninsula.

Legend about the Tauri

According to Greek legends, the Tauri were the people to whom Iphigeneia was sent after the goddess Artemis rescued her from her father Agamemnon, who was about to sacrifice her to appease Artemis. She became a priestess at the goddess's temple in the land of the Tauri, where she was forced by King Thoas to sacrifice any foreigners who came ashore.

The land of the Tauric Chersonese and custom of killing Greeks are described by Herodotus in his histories.

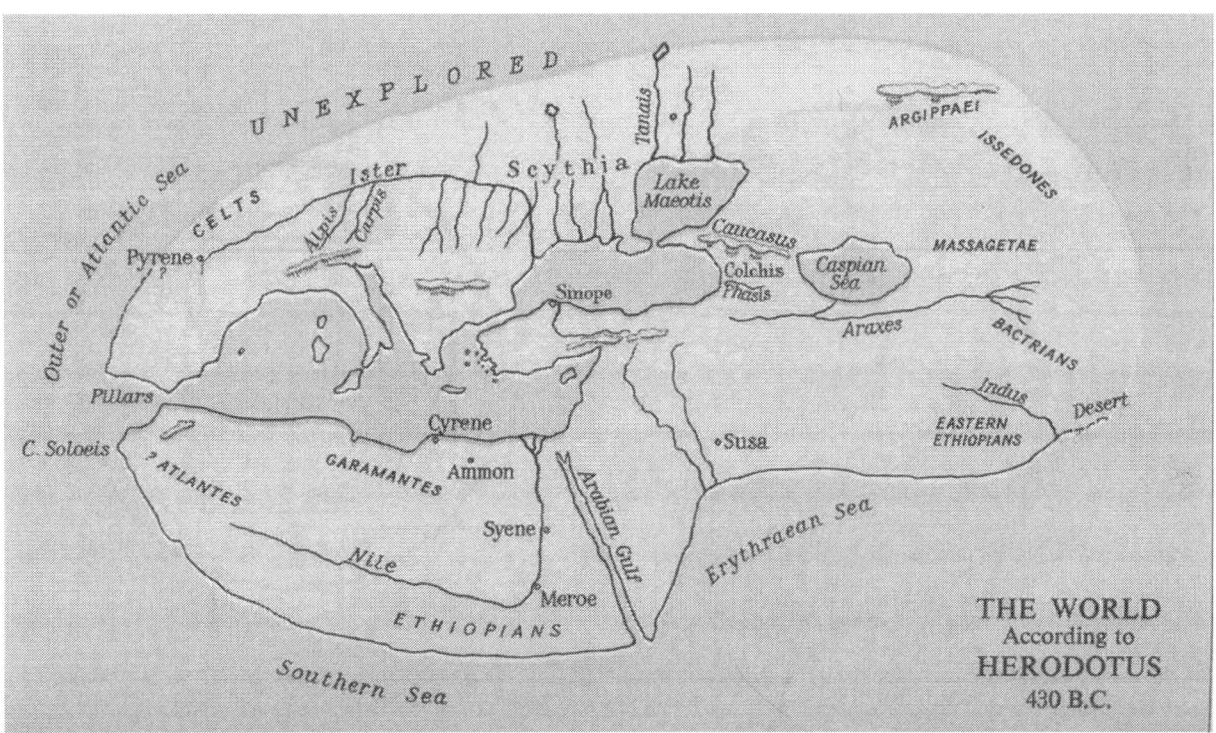

THE CIMMERIANS OR KIMMERIANS

The Tauric Chersonese was inhabited by a variety of peoples. The inland regions were inhabited by Scythians and the mountainous south coast by the Tauri, an offshoot of the Cimmerians, an ancient Indo-European people living north of the Caucasus and the Sea of Azov as early as 1300 BC until they were driven southward by the Scythians into Anatolia during the 8th century BC. Linguistically they are usually regarded as Iranian, or possibly Thracian with an Iranian ruling class.

After their exodus from the Pontic steppe the Cimmerians probably assaulted Urartu about 714 BC.

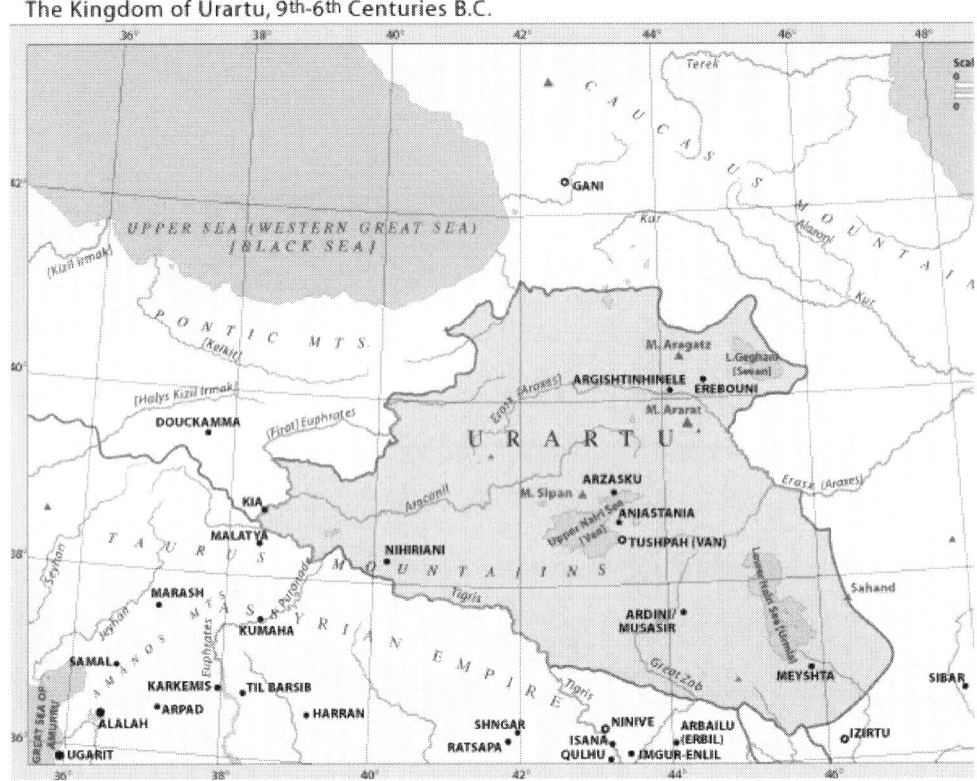

But in 705 BC, after being repulsed by Sargon II of Assyria, they turned towards Anatolia and in 696–695 conquered Phrygia. In 652, after taking Sardis, the capital of Lydia, they reached their height of power.

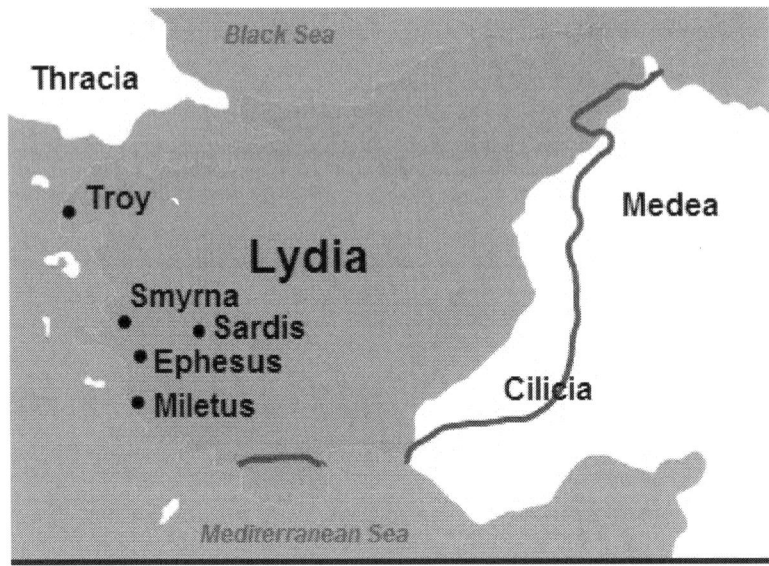

Their decline quickly began, and their final defeat is dated between 637 or 626 BC, when they were defeated by Alyattes of Lydia. Thereafter, they are no longer mentioned in historical sources but probably settled in Cappadocia.

SCYTHIANS

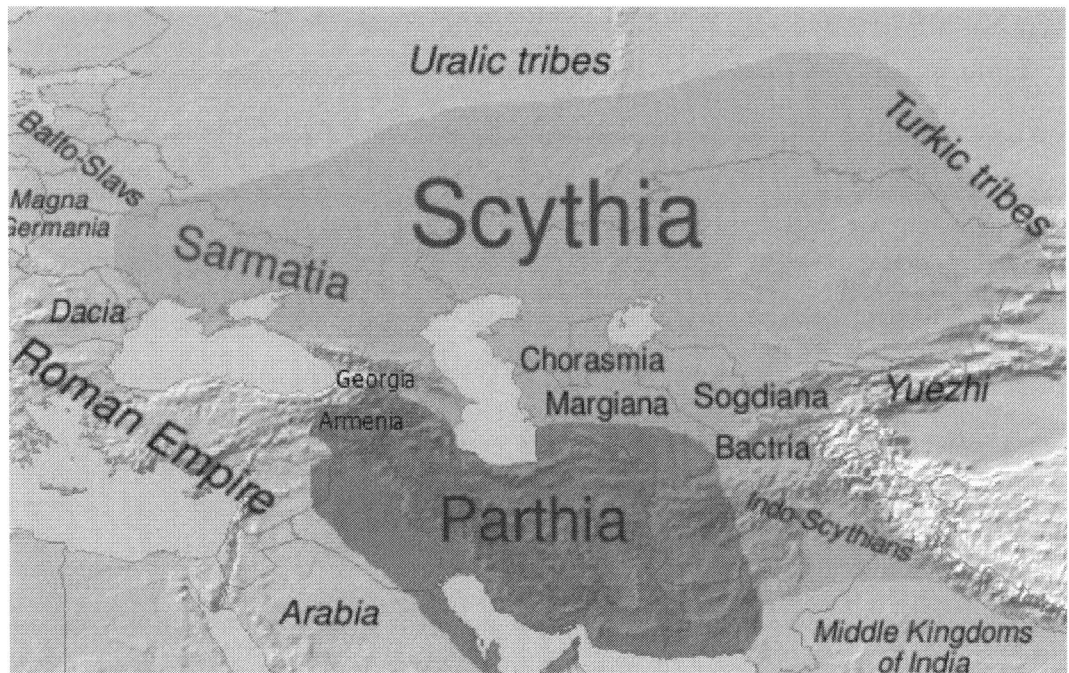

The Scythians were Iranic equestrian tribes who were mentioned as inhabiting large areas in the central Eurasian steppes starting with the 7th century BC up until the 4th century AD. Their territories during the Iron Age were known to classical Greek sources as "Scythia". Their historical appearance coincided with the rise of equestrian semi-nomadism from the Carpathian Mountains of Europe to Mongolia in the Far East during the 1st millennium BC. The "classical Scythians" known to ancient Greek historians were located in the northern Black Sea and fore-Caucasus region. However, other Scythian groups encountered in Near Eastern and Achaemenid sources existed in Central Asia.

Names

Herodotus provides a depiction that can be related to the results of archaeological research, but apparently knew little of the eastern part of Scythia. He did say that the ancient Persians called all the Scyths. The Chinese knew the Asian Scythians as Sai. Whether they adopted the Achaemenid name, or "Saka" came to be an endonym, it is not clear. The modern region of Sistan in eastern Iran and southern Afghanistan takes its name from the classical Sakastan (land of the Sakas)

Origins

The Scythians first appeared in the historical record in the 8th century BC. Herodotus reported three contradictory versions as to the origins of the Scythians, but placed greatest faith in this version: *The wandering Scythians once dwelt in Asia, and there warred with the Massagetae, but with ill success; they therefore quitted their homes, crossed the Araxes, and entered the land of Cimmeria.*

The term *Scythian*, like *Cimmerian*, was used to refer to a variety of groups from the Black Sea to southern Siberia and central Asia. They were not a specific people, but rather variety of peoples referred to at differing times in history, and in several places, none of which was their original homeland. The Bible includes a single reference to Scythians in Colossians 3:11:

Where there is neither Greek nor Jew, circumcision nor uncircumcision, Barbarian, Scythian, bond nor free: but Christ is all and in all.

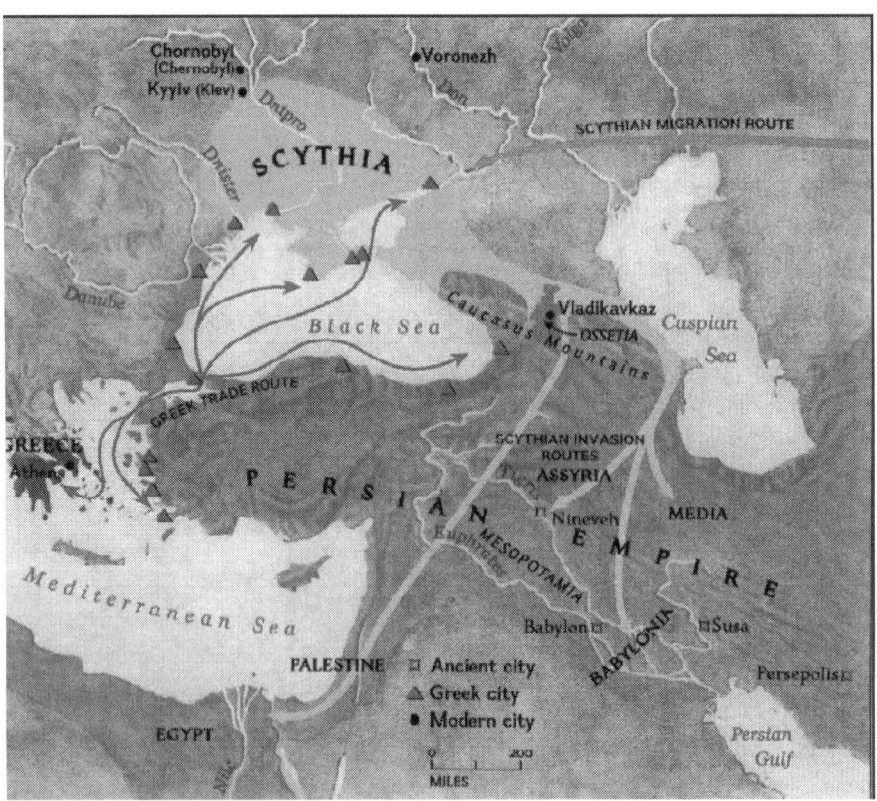

History: Classical Antiquity

Herodotus provides the first detailed description of the Scythians. He classes the Cimmerians as a distinct autochthonous tribe, expelled by the Scythians from the northern Black Sea coast. For Herodotus, the Scythians were outlandish barbarians living north of the Black Sea in what are now Moldova and Ukraine.

During the 5th to 3rd centuries BC, the Scythians evidently prospered. When Herodotus wrote his Histories in the 5th century BC, Greeks distinguished Scythia Minor, in present-day Romania and Bulgaria, from a Greater Scythia that extended eastwards for a 20-day ride from the Danube River, across the steppes of today's East Ukraine to the lower Don basin. The Don, then known as Tanaïs, has served as a major trading route ever since. The Scythians apparently obtained their wealth from their control over the slave trade from the north to Greece through the Greek Black Sea colonial ports of Olbia, Chersonesos, Cimmerian Bosporus, and Gorgippia. They also grew grain, and shipped wheat, flocks, and cheese to Greece.

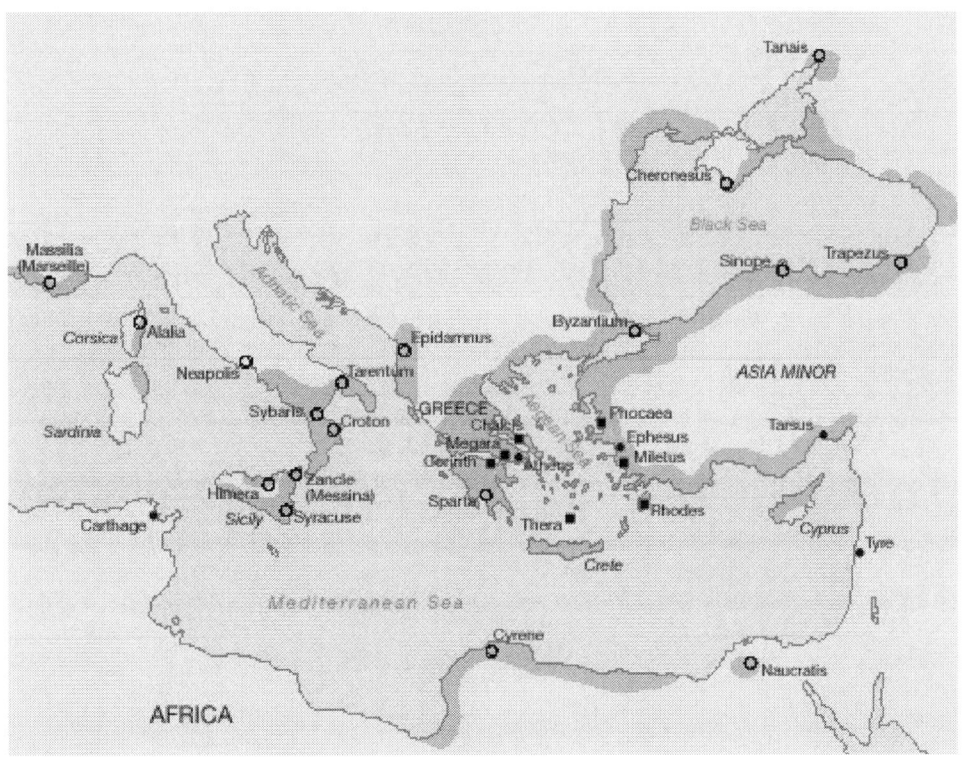

Greek Colonies in the Mediterranean and Black Sea

Warfare

The Scythians were notoriously aggressive warriors. They "fought to live and lived to fight" and "drank the blood of their enemies and used the scalps as napkins." Ruled by small numbers of closely allied élites, Scythians had a reputation for their archers, and many gained employment as mercenaries.

Strabo (c. 63 BC – 24 AD) reports that King Ateas united under his power the Scythian tribes living between the Maeotian marshes and the Danube. His westward expansion brought him into conflict with Philip II of Macedon (reigned 359 to 336 BC), who took military action against the Scythians in 339 BC. Ateas died in battle, and his empire disintegrated.

In the aftermath of this defeat, the Celts seem to have displaced the Scythians from the Balkans, whereas In south Russia, a kindred tribe, the Sarmatians, gradually overwhelmed them.

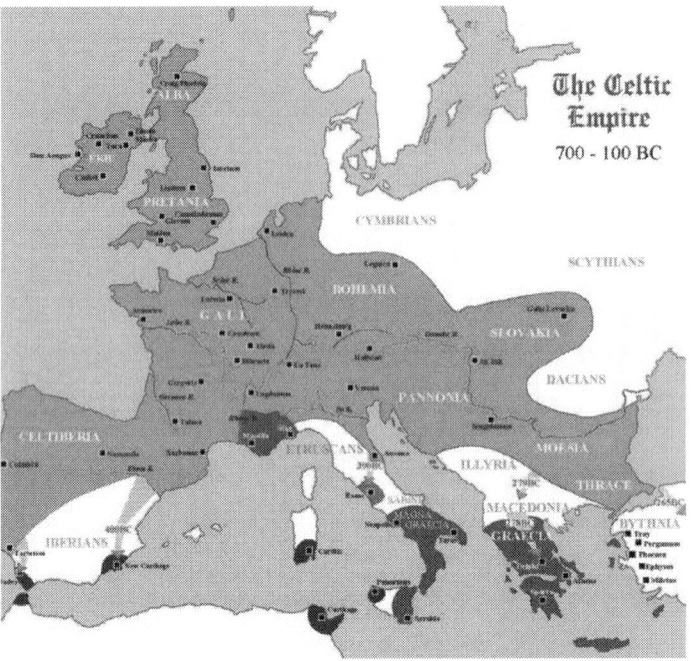

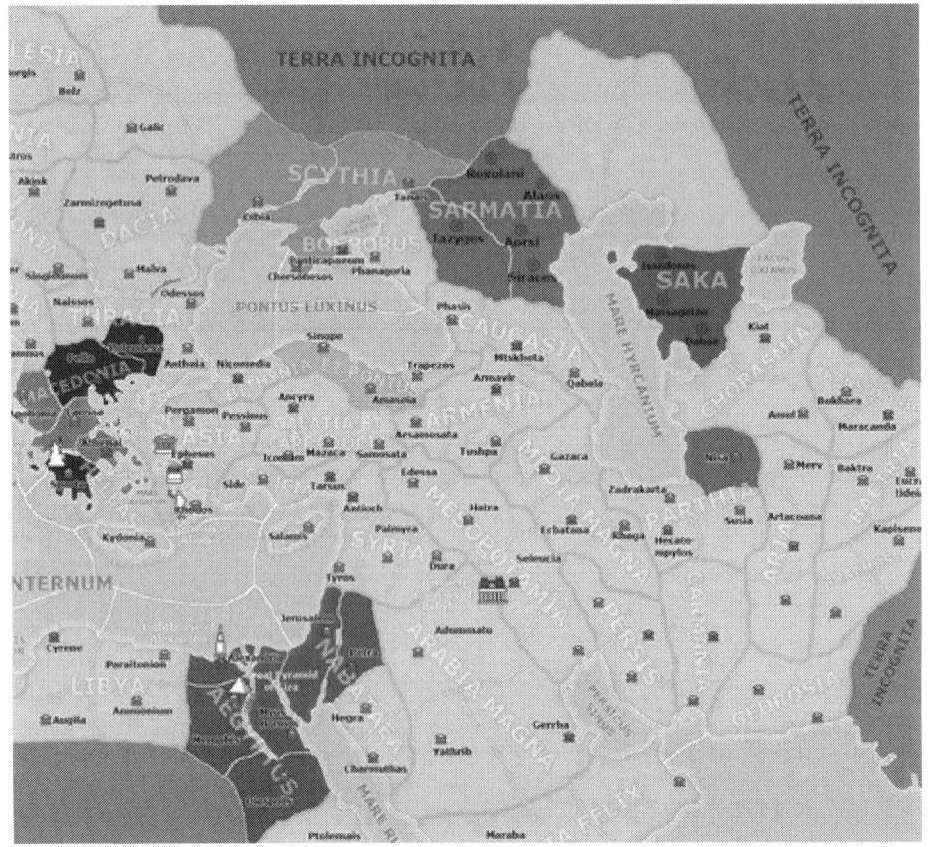

In 329 BC Philip's son, Alexander the Great, came into conflict with the Scythians at the Battle of Jaxartes. A Scythian army sought to take revenge against the Macedonians for the death of Ateas, as they pushed the borders of their empire north and east, and to take advantage of a revolt by the local Sogdiansatrap

Alexander did not intend to subdue the nomads: he wanted to go to the south, where a far more serious crisis demanded his attention. He could do so now without loss of face; and in order to make the outcome acceptable to the Saccae, he released the Scythian prisoners of war without ransom in order to broker a peace agreement. This policy was successful, and the Scythians no longer harassed Alexander's empire.

However, the Scythian army was defeated by Alexander at the Battle of Jaxartes.

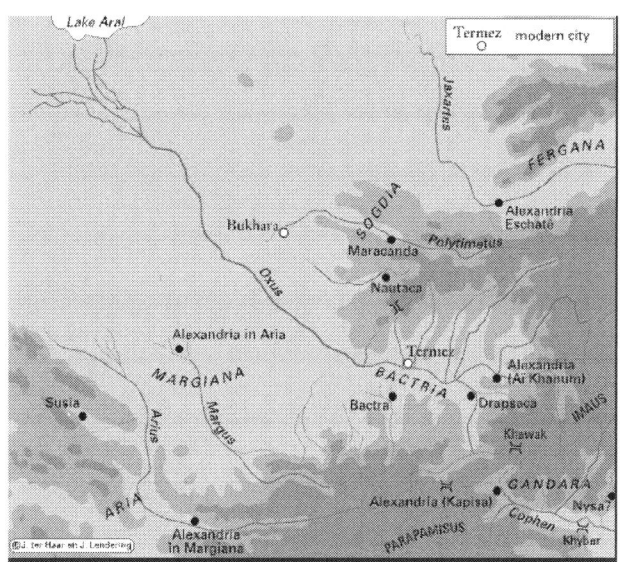

Alexander crossing the Jaxartes River

By the time of Strabo's account (the first decades AD), the Crimean Scythians had created a new kingdom extending from the lower Dnieper to the Crimea. The kings Skilurus and Palakus waged wars with Mithridates the Great (reigned 120–63 BC) for control of the Crimean littoral, including Chersonesos and the Cimmerian Bosporus. Their capital city, Scythian Neapolis, stood on the outskirts of modern Simferopol. The Goths destroyed it later, in the mid-3rd century AD.

LATE ANTIQUITY (AD 300 TO 600)

Sakas and Indo-Scythians

In Late Antiquity, the notion of a Scythian ethnicity grew more vague and outsiders might dub any people inhabiting the Pontic-Caspian steppe as *Scythians*, regardless of their language. Thus, Priscus, a Byzantine emissary to Attila, repeatedly referred to the latter's followers as *Scythians*.

Goths had displaced the Sarmatians in the 2nd century from most areas near the Roman frontier.

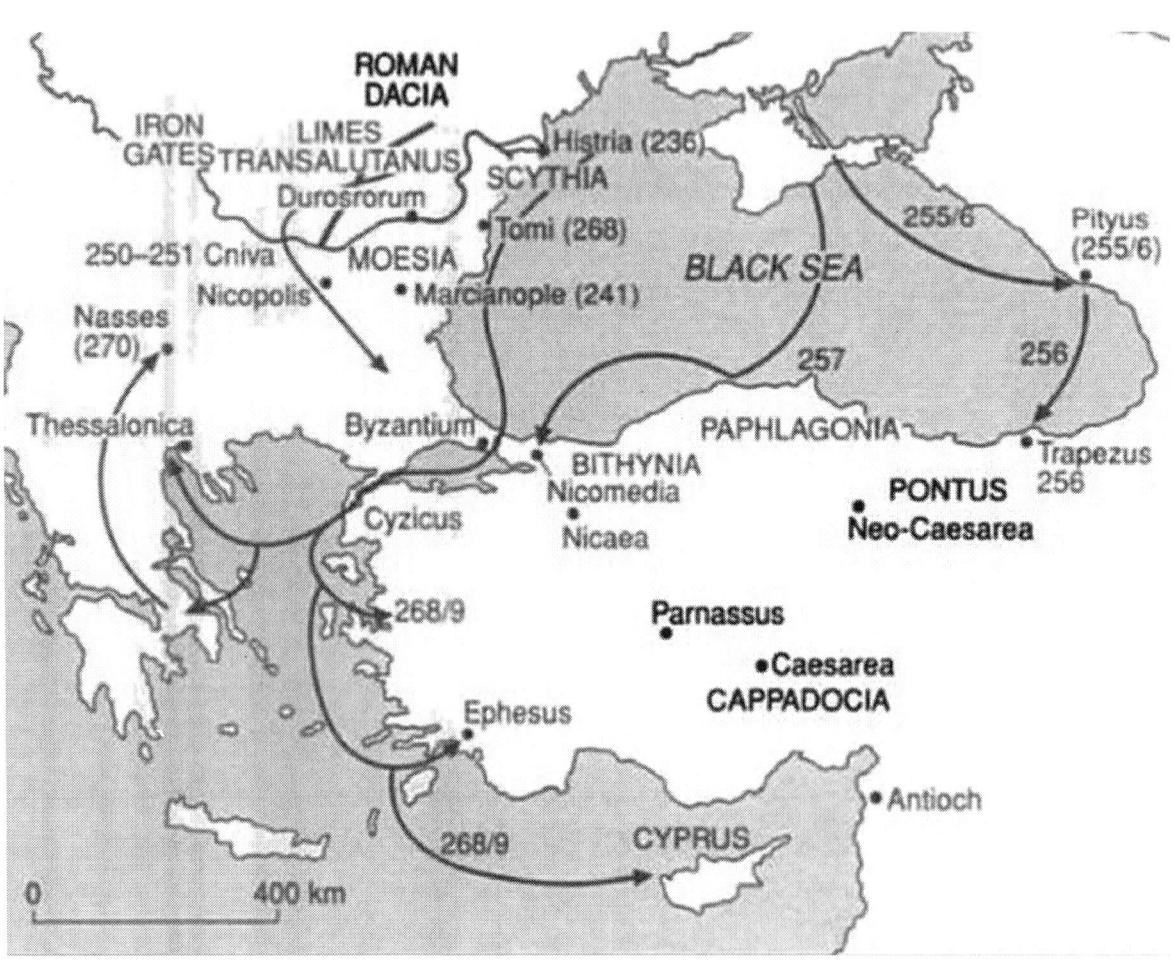

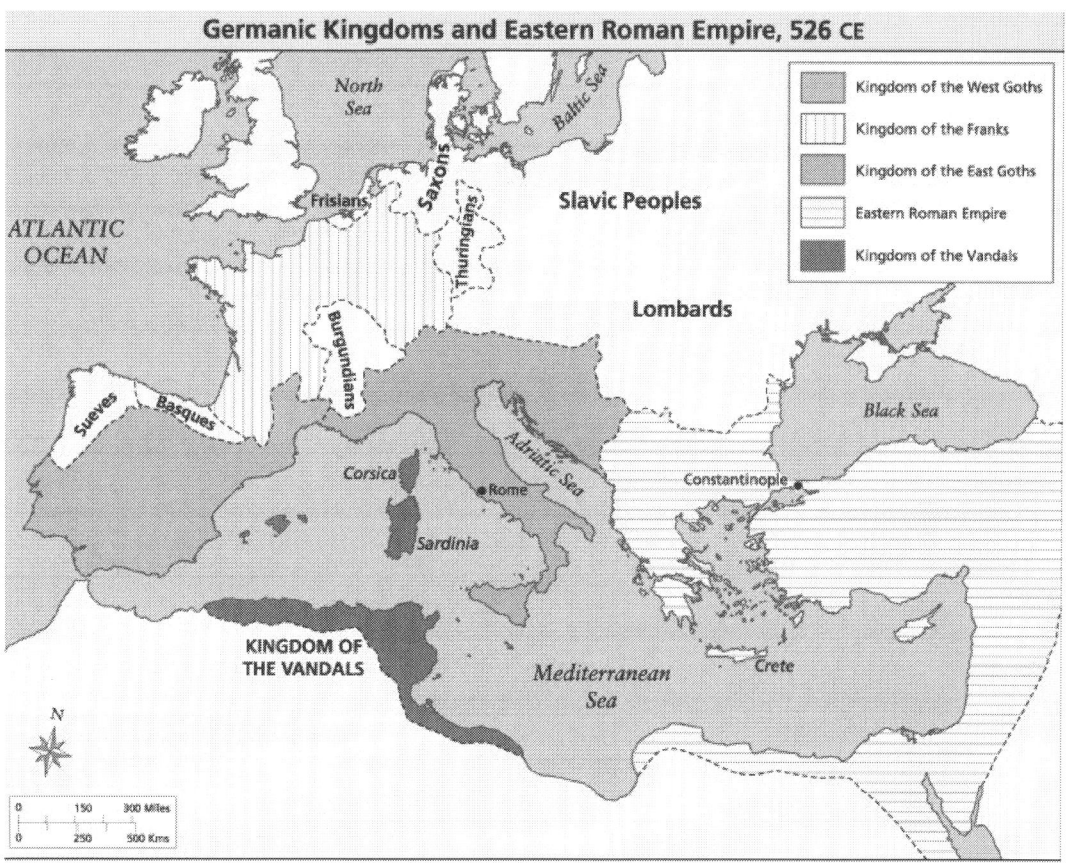

the Turkic migration marginalized East Iranian dialects, and assimilated the Saka linguistically.

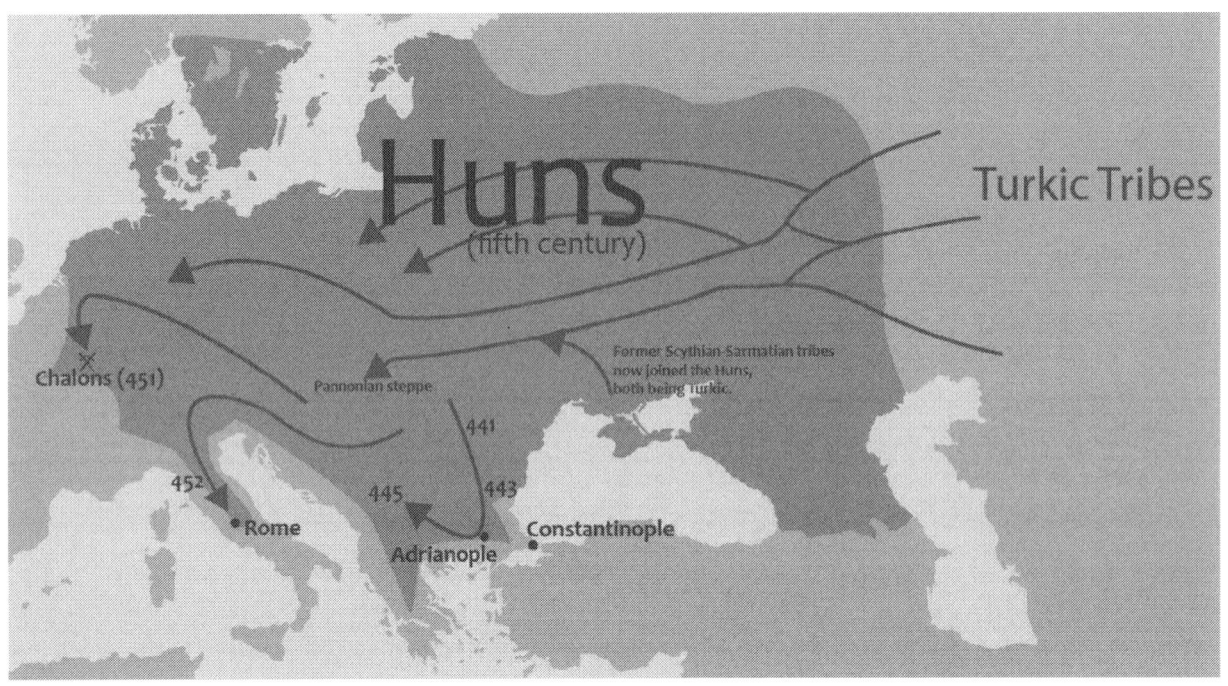
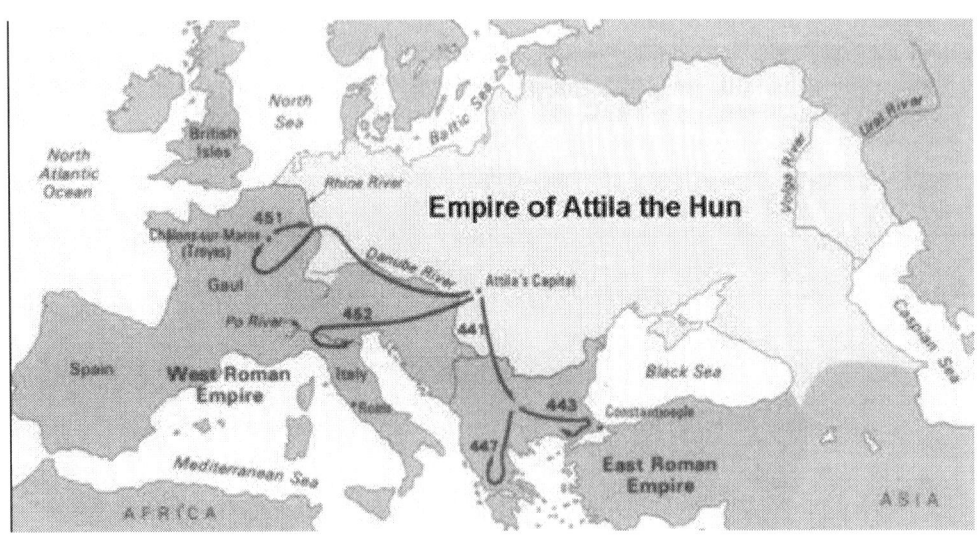

Greek settlers

Greeks established a number of colonies along the coast of the peninsula, notably the city of Chersonesus near modern Sevastopol.

 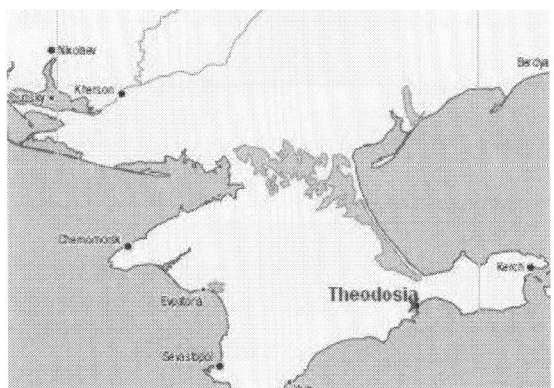

According to Diodorus Siculus , the region was governed from 480 BC to 438 BC by a line called the Archaeanactidae, probably a ruling family, which gave way to the tyrant Spartocus (438 BC - 431 BC), apparently a Thracian. He founded a dynasty which seems to have endured until around 110 BC. The Spartocids have left many inscriptions which indicate that the earlier members of the house ruled as archons of the Greek cities and kings of various native tribes, notably the Sindi of the island district and other branches of the Maeotae. The texts, inscriptions and coins do not supply sufficient material for a complete list of these monarchs.

Satyrus (431 BC - 387 BC), Spartocus' successor, established his rule over the whole district, adding Nymphaeum to his dominions and laying siege to Theodosia, which was a serious commercial rival because of its ice-free port and proximity to the grain fields of eastern Crimea. It was reserved for his son Leucon (387 BC - 347 BC) to take this city. He was succeeded by his two sons conjointly, Spartocus II, and Paerisades; the former died in 342, and his brother reigned alone until 310 BC.

Then followed a civil war, in which Satyrus defeated his younger brother Eumelus at the Battle of the River Thatis in 310 BC, but then was killed, giving Eumelus the throne.

His successor was Spartocus III (303 BC - 283 BC) and after him Paerisades II. Succeeding princes repeated the family names, but no certain order can be assigned. It is known that the last of them, Paerisades V, unable to make headway against the power of the natives, in 108 BC called in the help of Diophantus, general of Mithridates the Great of Pontus, promising to hand over his kingdom to that prince. He was slain by a Scythian named Saumacus who led a rebellion against him.

The house of Spartocus was well known as a line of enlightened and wise princes; although Greek opinion could not deny that they were, strictly speaking, tyrants, they are always described as dynasts. They maintained close relations with Athens, their best customer for the Bosporan grain export, of which Leucon I set the staple at Theodosia, where the Attic ships were allowed special privileges. The Attic orators make numerous references to this. In return, the Athenians granted him citizenship and set up decrees in honour of him and his sons.

In the 2nd century BC, the eastern part of the Tauric Chersonese became part of the Bosporan Kingdom.

In the 1st century BC, after his defeat by Pompey in 63 BC, Mithradates VI, King of Pontus, fled with a small army from Colchis (modern Georgia) over the Caucasus Mountains to Crimea and made plans to raise yet another army to take on the Romans. His eldest living son, Machares, viceroy of Cimmerian Bosporus, was unwilling to aid his father.

Mithradates had Machares killed, and took the throne of the Bosporan Kingdom. Mithradates then ordered conscription and preparations for war. In 63 BC, Pharnaces II, his younger son, led a rebellion against his father, joined by Roman exiles in the core of Mithradates' Pontic army. Mithradates withdrew to the citadel in Panticapaeum, where he committed suicide the same year. Pompey the Great buried Mithradates in the rock-cut tombs of his ancestors in Amasya, the old capital of Pontus.

Mithridates (left), Pompey (right)

Roman Bosporan Kingdom

After the death of Mithridates, Pharnaces (63 BC - 47 BC) made his submission to Pompey, then tried to regain his dominion during the civil war, but was defeated by Caesar at Zela and later killed by a former governor of his. A pretender, Asander married his daughter Dynamis, and in spite of Roman nominees, ruled as archon, and later as king, until 17 BC. After his death, Dynamis was compelled to marry a Roman usurper called Scribonius, but the Romans under Agrippa interfered and set Polemon I of Pontus (16 BC - 8 BC) in his place. Dynamis died in 14 BC and Polemon ruled until 8 BC.

After Polemon's death, Tiberius Julius Aspurgus (8 BC - 38), son of Dynamis and Asander, succeeded him and founded a line of kings which endured with certain interruptions until 341 AD. Originally called Aspurgus, he adopted the names "Tiberius Augustus" because he enjoyed the patronage of the first two Roman emperors, Augustus and Tiberius. All of the following kings adopted these two Roman names followed by a third name, mostly of Pontic and Thracian origin.

As the dynasty descended from Mithridates VI through Aspurgus, the kings adopted the Pontic era introduced by Mithridates, which started with 297 BC; this era was used to date coins. Bosporan kings struck coinage throughout the kingdom period, which included gold staters bearing portraits of the respective Roman emperors. However this coinage became increasingly debased in the 3rd century. The rulers' names and dates are fairly well known, though scarcely any events of their reigns are recorded. Their kingdom covered the eastern half of Crimea and the Taman peninsula, and extended along the east coast of the Maeotian marshes to Tanais at the mouth of the Don, a great market for trade with the interior.

They carried on a perpetual war with the native tribes, and in this were supported by their Roman suzerains, who even lent the assistance of garrisons and fleets. In 63 AD, for unknown reasons, the Roman Emperor Nero deposed Tiberius Julius Cotys I from his throne: the Bosporan Kingdom became a Roman province from 63-68. In 68 AD, the new Roman emperor, Galba, restored the Bosporan Kingdom to Tiberius Julius Rhescuporis I.

During the 1st, 2nd, and 3rd centuries AD, Taurica was host to Roman legions and colonists in Charax. Charax was founded under Vespasian with the intention of protecting Chersonesus and other Bosporean trade centres from the Scythians. The Roman colony was protected by a vexillation of the Legio I Italica; it also hosted a detachment of the Legio XI Claudia at the end of the 2nd century. The camp was abandoned by the Romans in the mid-3rd century.

This de facto province would have been controlled by the legatus of one of the Legions stationed in Charax.

Taurica remained a vassal state of the Romans for nearly five centuries, and the southern shores remained under Byzantine control until the AD 13th century. At times, rival kings of some other races arose and probably produced some disorganization. At one of these periods (255), the Goths and Borani were able to seize Bosporan shipping and raid the shores of Anatolia.

With the coins of the last king, Tiberius Julius Rhescuporis VI, in 341 AD, materials for a connected history of the Bosporus Cimmerius came to an end. The kingdom probably succumbed to the Huns, who defeated the nearby Alans in 375/376 AD and moved rapidly westwards, bringing destruction in their wake.

CRIMEA IN THE MIDDLE AGES

Throughout the later centuries, Crimea was invaded or occupied successively by the Goths (AD 250),

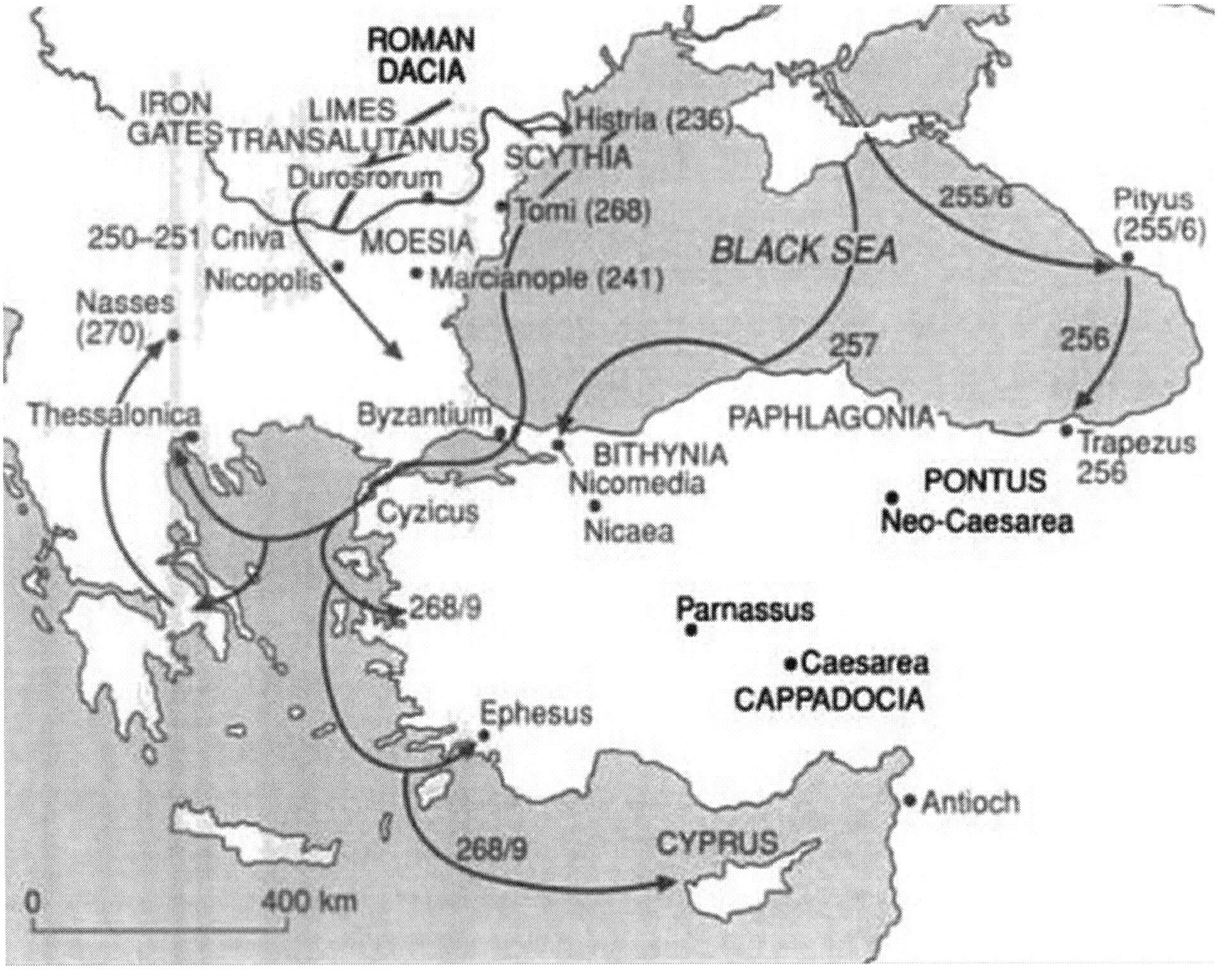

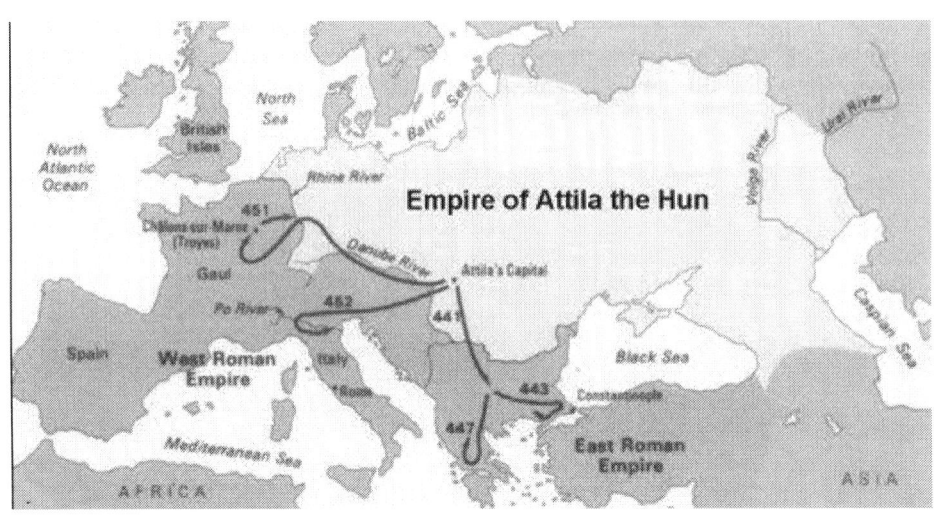

And the Huns (376),

And the Bulgars (4th–8th century),

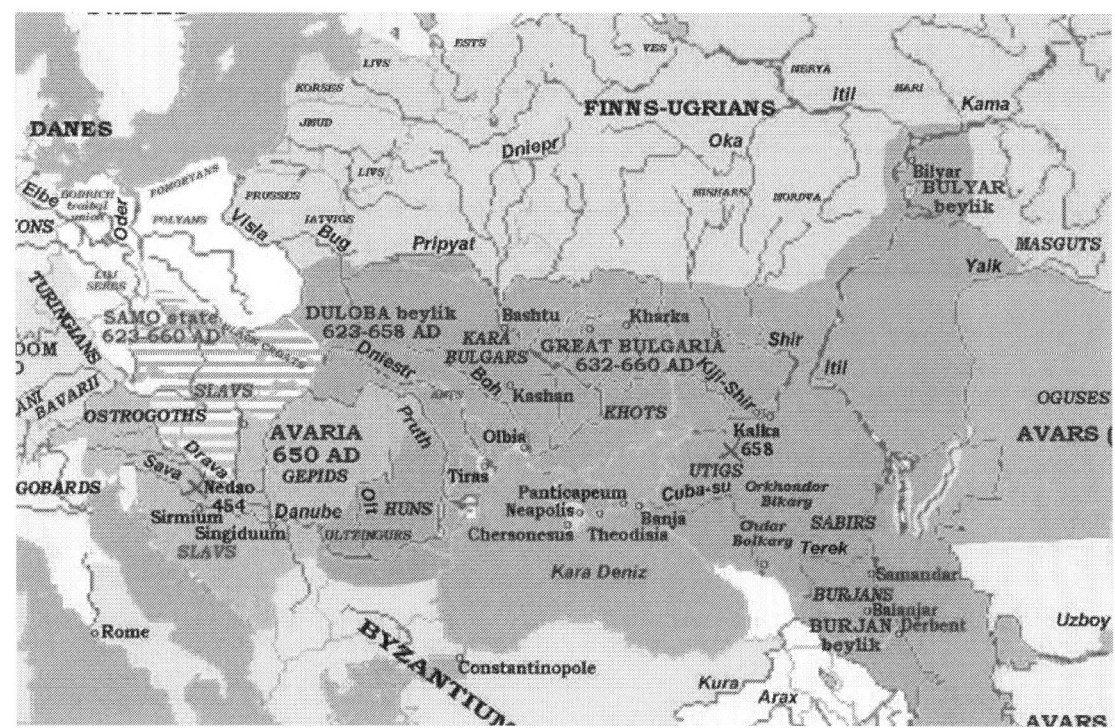

And the Khazars (8th century),

and the state of Kievan Rus' (10th–11th centuries), and the Byzantine Empire (1016)

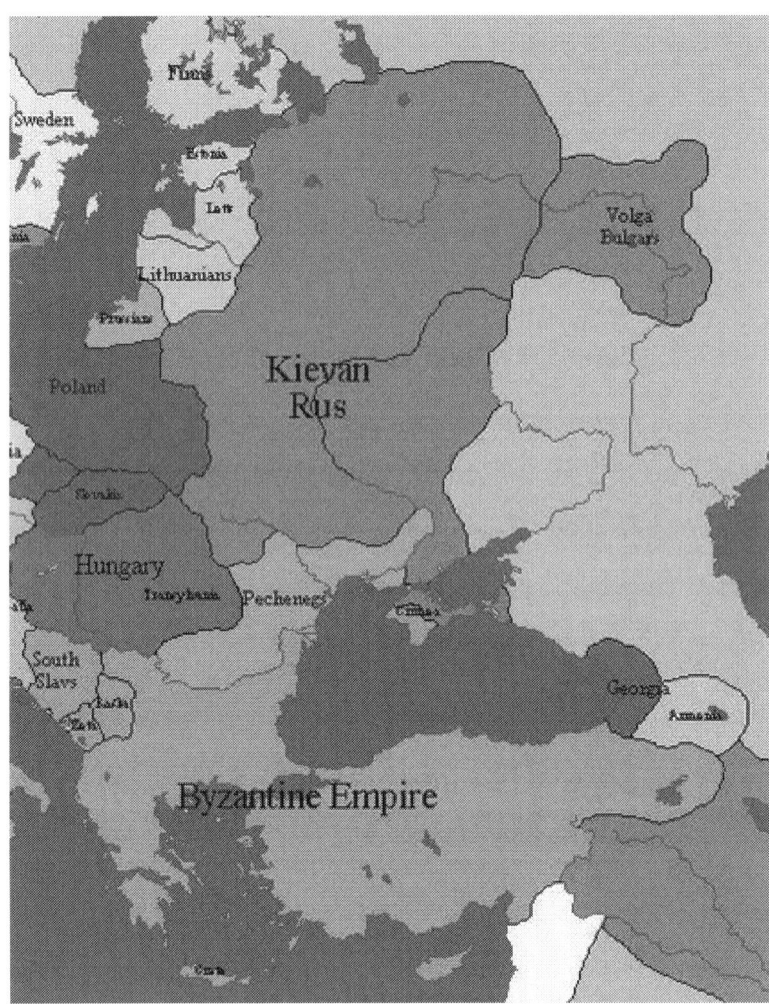

In the mid-10th century, the eastern area of Crimea was conquered by Prince Sviatoslav I of Kiev and became part of the Kievan Rus' principality of Tmutarakan. In 988, Prince Vladimir I of Kiev also captured the Byzantine town of Chersonesos (presently part of Sevastopol) where he later converted to Christianity. An impressive Russian Orthodox cathedral marks the location of this historic event.

They were followed by the Kipchaks (Kumans) (1050)

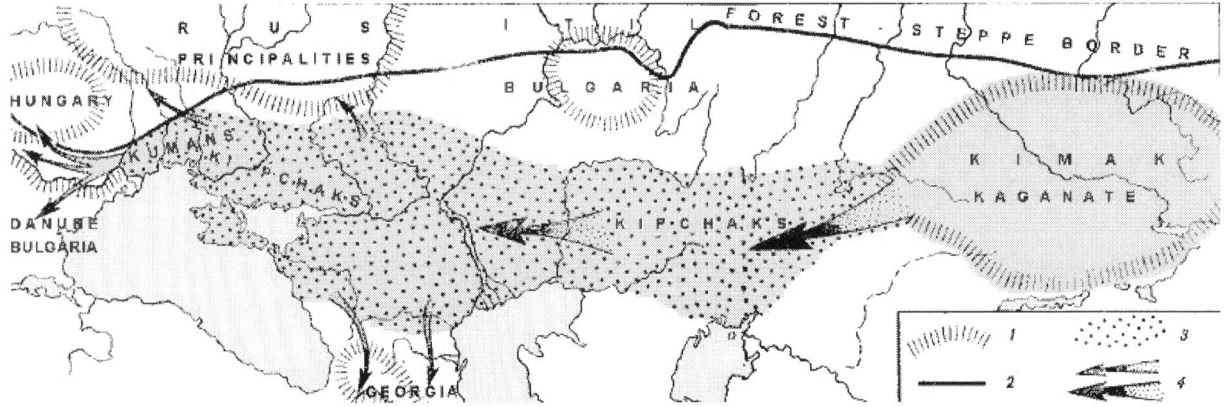

and the Mongols (1237).

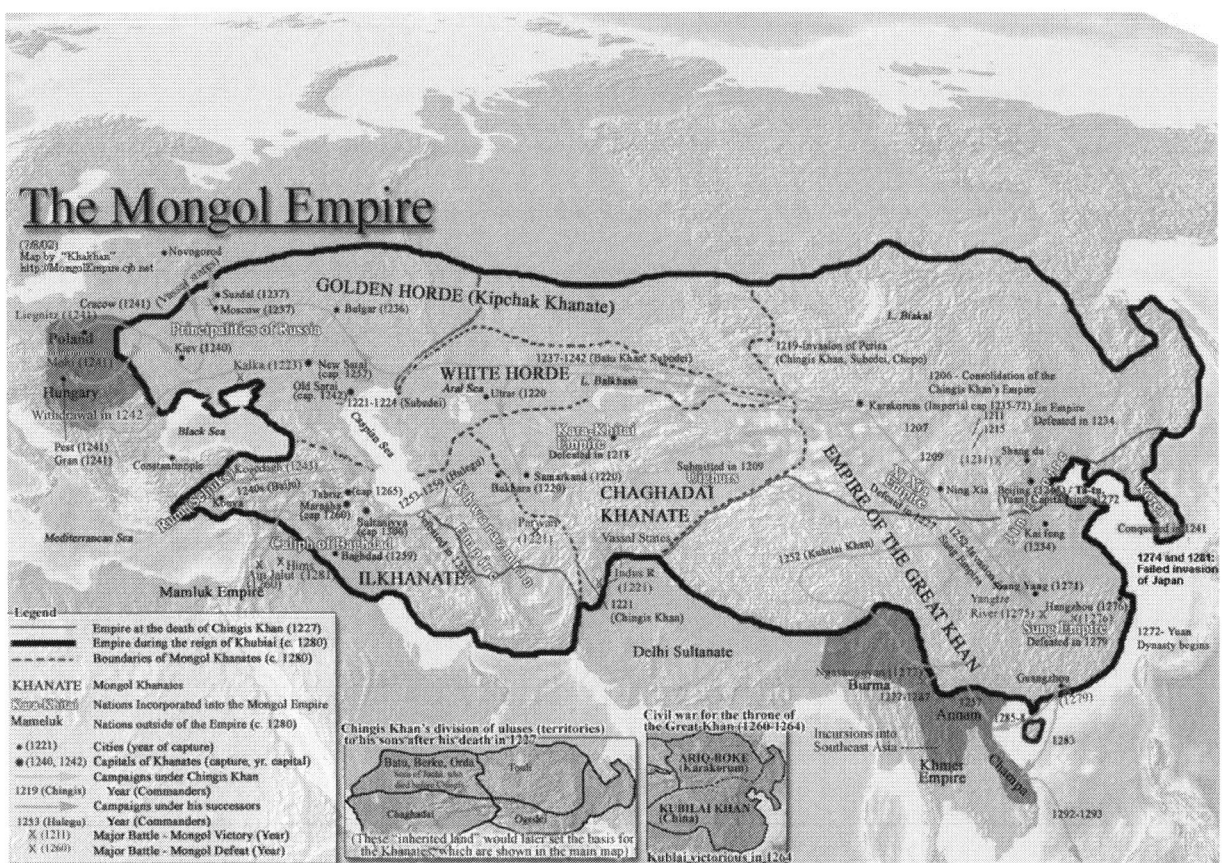

In the 13th century, the Republic of Genoa seized the settlements which their rivals, the Venetians, had built along the Crimean coast and established themselves at Cembalo (now Balaklava), Soldaia (Sudak), Cherco (Kerch) and Caffa (Feodosiya), gaining control of the Crimean economy and the Black Sea commerce for two centuries.

CRIMEAN KHANATE: 1441–1783

A number of Turkic peoples, now collectively known as the Crimean Tatars, have been inhabiting the peninsula since the early Middle Ages. The ethnicity of the Crimean Tatars is quite complex as it absorbed both nomadic Turkic and European components (including, at first, the Goths and the Genoese) which is still reflected in their appearance and language differences. A small enclave of the Karaylar, generally believed to be of Khazar (i.e. Turkic) descent practising Karaism, was founded in the 8th century. It existed among the Muslim Crimean Tatars, primarily in the mountainous Çufut Qale area.

In 1346, the bodies of Mongol warriors of the Golden Horde who had died of plague were thrown over the walls of the besieged Kaffa (now Feodosiya). It has been speculated that this operation may have been responsible for the advent of the Black Death in Europe.

After the destruction of the Mongolian Golden Horde by Timur in 1441, the Crimean Tatars founded an independent Crimean Khanate under Hacı I Giray, a descendant of Genghis Khan who was Mongol leader. He and his successors reigned first at Qırq Yer, and from the beginning of the 15th century, at Bakhchisaray.

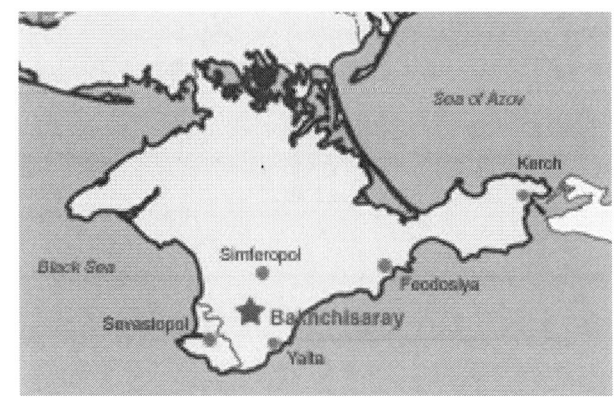

The Crimean Tatars controlled the steppes that stretched from the Kuban and to the Dniester River, however, they were unable to take control over commercial Genoese towns. After the Crimean Tatars asked for help from the Ottomans, an Ottoman invasion of the Genoese towns led by Gedik Ahmed Pasha in 1475 brought Kaffa and the other trading towns under their control.

After the capture of Genoese towns, the Ottoman Sultan held Meñli I Giray captive, later releasing him in return for accepting Ottoman suzerainty over the Crimean Khans and allowing them rule as tributary princes of the Ottoman Empire. However, the Crimean Khans still had a large amount of autonomy from the Ottoman Empire, particularly, followed the rules they thought were best for them: Crimean Tatars introduced raids into Ukrainian lands, which were used to get slaves to be sold on markets. For example, from 1450 to 1586, eighty-six Tatar raids were recorded, and from 1600 to 1647, seventy. In the 1570s close to 20,000 slaves a year were being sold in Kaffa.

Tartaren aus der Krimm.

Cossacks

There is hardly a single simple definition for them. They are not a nationality or a religion, they don't represent a political party or movement and there is still no complete agreement among historians and anthropologists on who the Cossacks are.

Described in a few words, Cossacks are free men or adventurers. In fact, their name is derived from the Turkish *Qasaq*, which means exactly that.

There are different versions of the origin of the Cossacks. According to some historians, in Russia and Ukraine Cossacks were the men who lived freely on the outlying districts. Usually they were serfs who had run away to find their own freedom.

The government tried to find and punish them, but the number of those on the run became so great that it was impossible to catch them all and soon the state had to give up and recognize the newly established communities on its borders. The first such self-governing warrior Cossack communities were formed in the 15th century (or, according to some sources, in the 13th century) in the Dnieper and Don River regions.

Cossacks also accepted Tatars, Germans, Turks and other nationalities into their communities, but there was one condition – they had to believe in Christ. Once accepted into the community, they stopped being Germans, Russians or Ukrainians – they became Cossacks.

Cossacks had their own elected headman, called ataman, who had executive powers and was supreme commander during the war. Rada (the Band Assembly) held the legislative powers. The senior officers were called *starshina* and the Cossack settlements were called *stanitsas*. The Cossacks were named by their geographical locations, some of the most famous ones were the Zaporozhian, Don and Kuban Cossacks.

In 1553–1554, Cossack Hetman Dmytro Vyshnevetsky gathered together groups of Cossacks, and constructed a fort designed to obstruct Tatar raids into Ukraine. With this action, he founded the Zaporozhian Sich, with which he would launch a series of attacks on the Crimean Peninsula and the Ottoman Turks. In 1774, the Crimean Khans fell under Russian influence with the Treaty of Küçük Kaynarca. In 1778, numerous Greek Orthodox residents were deported from Crimea to the vicinity of Mariupol by the Russian government. In 1783, the entire Crimea was annexed by the Russian Empire.

The Crimean Tatars discovered their ethnic identity on the Crimean Peninsula. The Khanate of the Crimea was founded in 1443 as a remnant of the Golden Horde. The Crimean Khanate exercised considerable power in eastern Europe from the beginning of the 16th century up until the end of the 17th. For centuries it had an alliance with Turkey.

Russo-Turkish wars

There was a series of wars between Russia and the Ottoman Empire in the 17th–19th century. The wars reflected the decline of the Ottoman Empire and resulted in the gradual southward extension of Russia's frontier and influence into Ottoman territory. The wars took place in 1676–81, 1687, 1689, 1695–96, 1710–12 (part of the Great Northern War), 1735–39, 1768–74, 1787–91, 1806–12, 1828–29, 1853–56 (part of the Crimean War), and 1877–78. As a result of these wars, Russia was able to extend its European frontiers southward to the Black Sea, southwestward to the Prut River, and south of the Caucasus Mountains in Asia.

The early Russo-Turkish Wars were mostly sparked by Russia's attempts to establish a warm-water port on the Black Sea, which lay in Turkish hands. The first war (1676–81) was fought without success in Ukraine west of the Dnieper River by Russia, which renewed the war with failed invasions of the Crimea in 1687 and 1689. In the war of 1695–96, the Russian tsar Peter I the Great's forces succeeded in capturing the fortress of Azov.

Peter the Great (left) and Capture of the Fortress of Azov by Cossacks (right)

In 1710 Turkey entered the Northern War against Russia, and after Peter the Great's attempt to liberate the Balkans from Ottoman rule ended in defeat at the Prut River (1711), he was forced to return Azov to Turkey. War again broke out in 1735, with Russia and Austria in alliance against Turkey. The Russians successfully invaded Turkish-held Moldavia, but their Austrian allies were defeated in the field, and as a result the Russians obtained almost nothing in the Treaty of Belgrade (Sept. 18, 1739).

The first major Russo-Turkish War (1768–74) began after Turkey demanded that Russia's ruler, Catherine II the Great, abstain from interfering in Poland's internal affairs. The Russians went on to win impressive victories over the Turks. They captured Azov, the Crimea, and Bessarabia, and under Field Marshal P.A. Rumyantsev they overran Moldavia and also defeated the Turks in Bulgaria. The Turks were compelled to seek peace, which was concluded in the Treaty of Küçük Kaynarca (July 21, 1774).

This treaty made the Crimean khanate independent of the Turkish sultan; advanced the Russian frontier southward to the Southern (Pivdennyy) Buh River; gave Russia the right to maintain a fleet on the Black Sea; and assigned Russia vague rights of protection over the Ottoman sultan's Christian subjects throughout the Balkans.

Catherine the Great

Russia was now in a much stronger position to expand, and in 1783 Catherine annexed the Crimean Peninsula outright. War broke out in 1787, with Austria again on the side of Russia (until 1791). Under General A.V. Suvorov, the Russians won several victories that gave them control of the lower Dniester and Danube rivers, and further Russian successes compelled the Turks to sign the Treaty of Jassy (Iași) on Jan. 9, 1792. By this treaty Turkey ceded the entire western Ukrainian Black Sea coast (from the Kerch Strait westward to the mouth of the Dniester) to Russia.

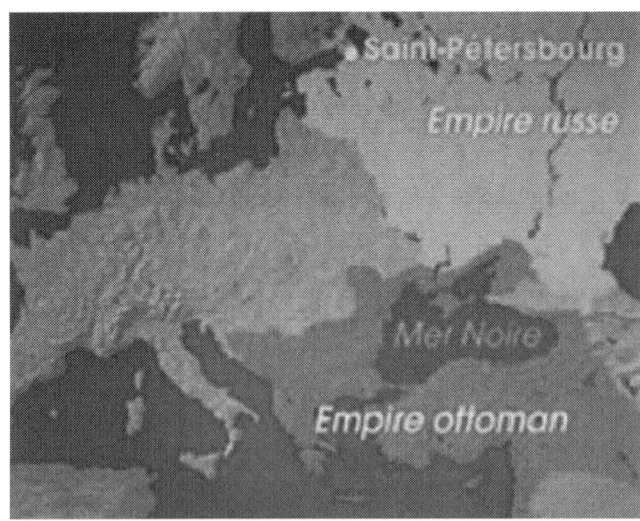

When Turkey deposed the Russophile governors of Moldavia and Walachia in 1806, war broke out again, though in a desultory fashion, since Russia was reluctant to concentrate large forces against Turkey while its relations with Napoleonic France were so uncertain. But in 1811, with the prospect of a Franco-Russian war in sight, Russia sought a quick decision on its southern frontier. The Russian field marshal M.I. Kutuzov's victorious campaign of 1811–12 forced the Turks to cede Bessarabia to Russia by the Treaty of Bucharest (May 28, 1812).

In 1783, after numerous wars between Russia and Turkey for control of the Black Sea, the Khanate was annexed by Russia. At that time the Crimean Tatars constituted 98 % of the population. In the 19th century the Crimea became the Russian's Black Sea bridgehead.

After the annexation of Crimea in 1783, the newly installed Russian authorities made an attempt to revive the ancient name, and the former lands of the Crimean Khanate were organized into the Taurida Governorate. But this name was used only in the official documents and "Crimea" remained a common name for the country.

The Taurida Oblast was created by a decree of Catherine the Great on 2 February 1784.

The center of the oblast was first in Karasubazar but was moved to Simferopol later in 1784. The establishment decree divided the oblast into 7 uyezds. However, by a decree of Paul I on 12 December 1796, the oblast was abolished and the territory, divided into 2 uyezds (Akmechetsky [Акмечетский] and Perekopsky [Перекопский]) was attached to the second incarantion of the Novorossiysk Governorate. At that time, there were 1,400 inhabited villages and 7 towns—Simferopol, Sevastopol, Yalta, Yevpatoria, Alushta, Feodosiya, and Kerch.

In 1802, in the course of Paul I's administrative reform of areas that were annexed from the Crimean Khanate, the Novorossiysk Governorate was again abolished and subdivided. Crimea was attached to a new Taurida Governorate established with its centre at Simferopol. The governorate included both the 25,133 km² Crimea as well as 38,405 km² of adjacent areas of the mainland.

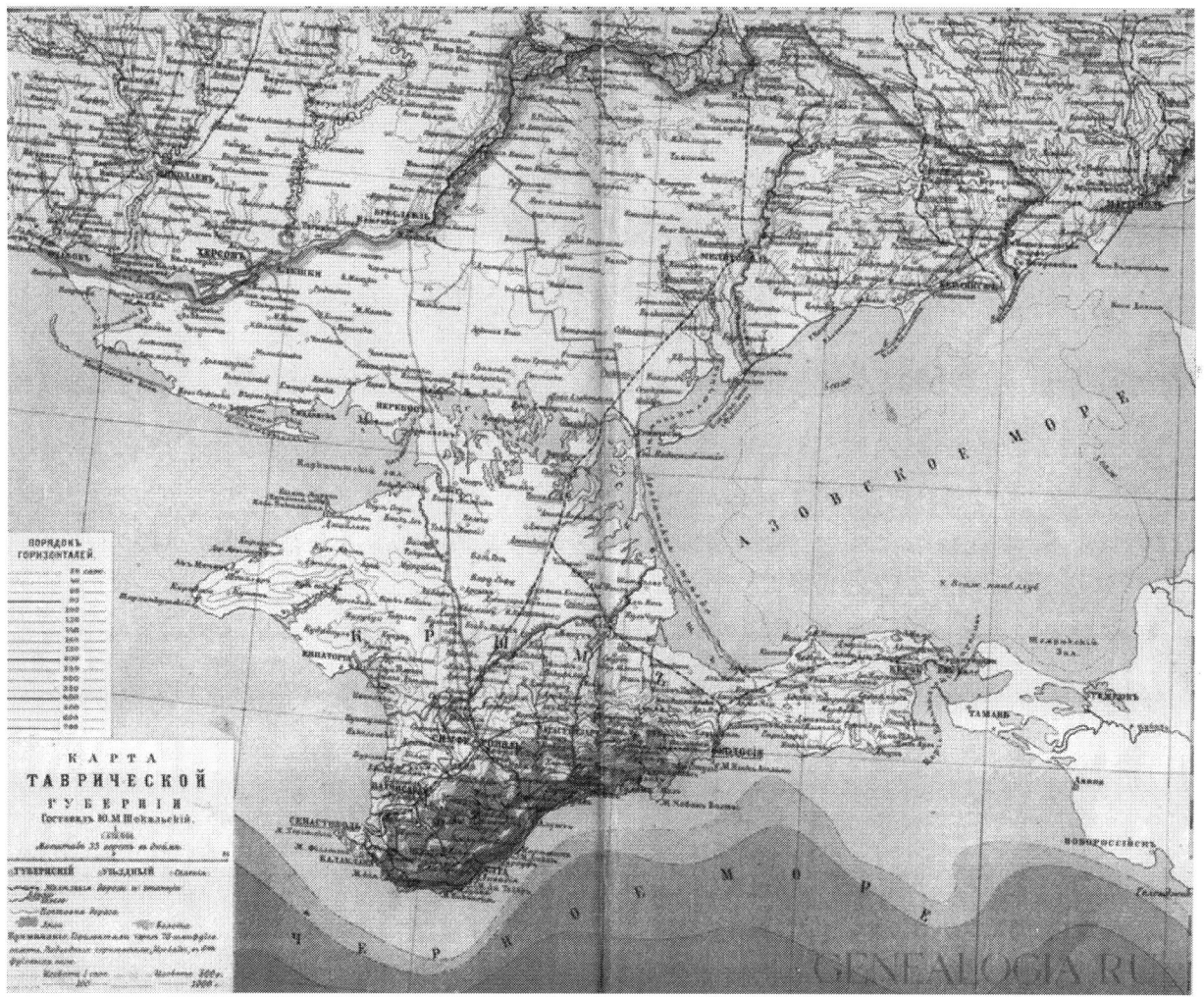

The expropriation of land and deportations, especially in the 1850s and 60s, forced a large number of Crimean Tatars to emigrate to Turkey. At the same time an influx of Russians began. By the late 19th century, Crimean Tatars continued to form a slight plurality of Crimea's still largely rural population but there were large numbers of Russians and Ukrainians as well as smaller numbers of Germans, Jews (including Krymchaks and Crimean Karaites), Bulgarians, Belarussians, Turks, Armenians, and Greeks and Gypsies.

The Tatars were the predominant portion of the population in the mountainous area and about half of the steppe population. Russians were concentrated most heavily in Feodosiya district. Germans and Bulgarians settled in the

Crimea at the beginning of 19th century, receiving a large allotment and fertile land and later wealthy colonists began to buy land, mainly in Perekopsky and Evpatoria uyezds.

Crimean War (October 1853–February 1856)

Fought mainly on the Crimean Peninsula between the Russians and the British, French, and Ottoman Turkish, with support from January 1855 by the army of Sardinia-Piedmont. The war arose from the conflict of great powers in the Middle East and was more directly caused by Russian demands to exercise protection over the Orthodox subjects of the Ottoman sultan. Another major factor was the dispute between Russia and France over the privileges of the Russian Orthodox and Roman Catholic churches in the holy places in Palestine.

Supported by Britain, the Turks took a firm stand against the Russians, who occupied the Danubian principalities (modern Romania) on the Russo-Turkish border in July 1853. The British fleet was ordered to Constantinople (Istanbul) on September 23. On October 4 the Turks declared war on Russia and in the same month opened an offensive against the Russians in the Danubian principalities. After the Russian Black Sea fleet destroyed a Turkish squadron at Sinope, on the Turkish side of the Black Sea, the British and French fleets entered the Black Sea on January 3, 1854, to protect Turkish transports. On March 28 Britain and France declared war on Russia. To satisfy Austria and avoid having that country also enter the war, Russia evacuated the Danubian principalities. Austria occupied them in August 1854. In September 1854 the allies landed troops in Russian Crimea, on the north shore of the Black Sea, and began a yearlong siege of the Russian fortress of Sevastopol. Major engagements were fought at the Alma River on September 20, at Balaklava on October 25 (commemorated in "The Charge of the Light Brigade" by English poet Alfred, Lord Tennyson), and at Inkerman on November 5. On January 26, 1855, Sardinia-Piedmont entered the war and sent 10,000 troops. Finally, on September 11, 1855, three days after a successful French assault on the Malakhov, a major strongpoint in the Russian defenses, the Russians blew up the forts, sank the ships, and evacuated Sevastopol. Secondary operations of the war were conducted in the Caucasus and in the Baltic Sea.

After Austria threatened to join the allies, Russia accepted preliminary peace terms on February 1, 1856. The Congress of Paris worked out the final settlement from February 25 to March 30. The resulting Treaty of Paris, signed on March 30, 1856, guaranteed the integrity of Ottoman Turkey and obliged Russia to surrender southern Bessarabia, at the mouth of the Danube. The Black Sea was neutralized, and the Danube River was opened to the shipping of all nations.

The Crimean War was managed and commanded very poorly on both sides. Disease accounted for a disproportionate number of the approximately 250,000 men lost by each side, although improvements made to the field hospital at Üsküdar by British nurse Florence Nightingale revolutionized the treatment of wounded soldiers and paved the way for later developments in battlefield medicine.

The war did not settle the relations of the powers in eastern Europe. It did awaken the new Russian emperor Alexander II (who succeeded Nicholas I in March 1855) to the need to overcome Russia's backwardness in order to compete successfully with the other European powers. A further result of the war was that Austria, having sided with Great Britain and France, lost the support of Russia in central European affairs. Austria became dependent on Britain and France, which failed to support that country, leading to the Austrian defeats in 1859 and 1866 that, in turn, led to the unification of Italy and of Germany..

The war devastated much of the economic and social infrastructure of Crimea. The Crimean Tatars had to flee from their homeland en masse, forced by the conditions created by the war, persecution and land expropriations.

Those who survived the trip, famine and disease, resettled in Dobruja, Anatolia, and other parts of the Ottoman Empire. Finally, the Russian government decided to stop the process, as the agriculture began to suffer due to the unattended fertile farmland.

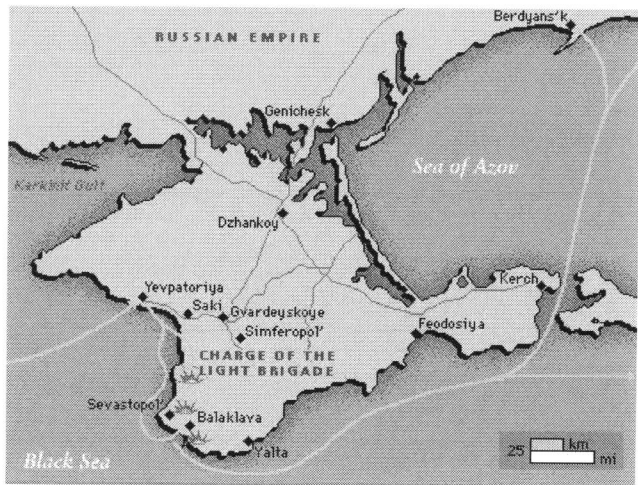

Charge of the Light Brigade

Florence Nightingale and wounded soldiers

Crimea in the Russian Civil War: 1917–1921

Following the 1917 October Revolution, the Taurida Governorate was briefly reformed as the Taurida Soviet Socialist Republic in early 1918 before being overrun by the World War I Central Powers. After the reassertion of Soviet control in 1921, the governorate was divided between the peninsular Crimean Autonomous Soviet Socialist Republic under the Russian SFSR and the mainland portions which were incorporated into the Ukrainian SSR.

Following the Russian Revolution of 1917, the military and political situation in Crimea was chaotic like that in much of Russia. During the ensuing Russian Civil War, Crimea changed hands numerous times and was for a time a stronghold of the anti-Bolshevik White Army. It was in Crimea that the White Russians led by General Wrangel made their last stand against Nestor Makhno and the Red Army in 1920. When resistance was crushed, many of the anti-Communist fighters and civilians escaped by ship to Istanbul.

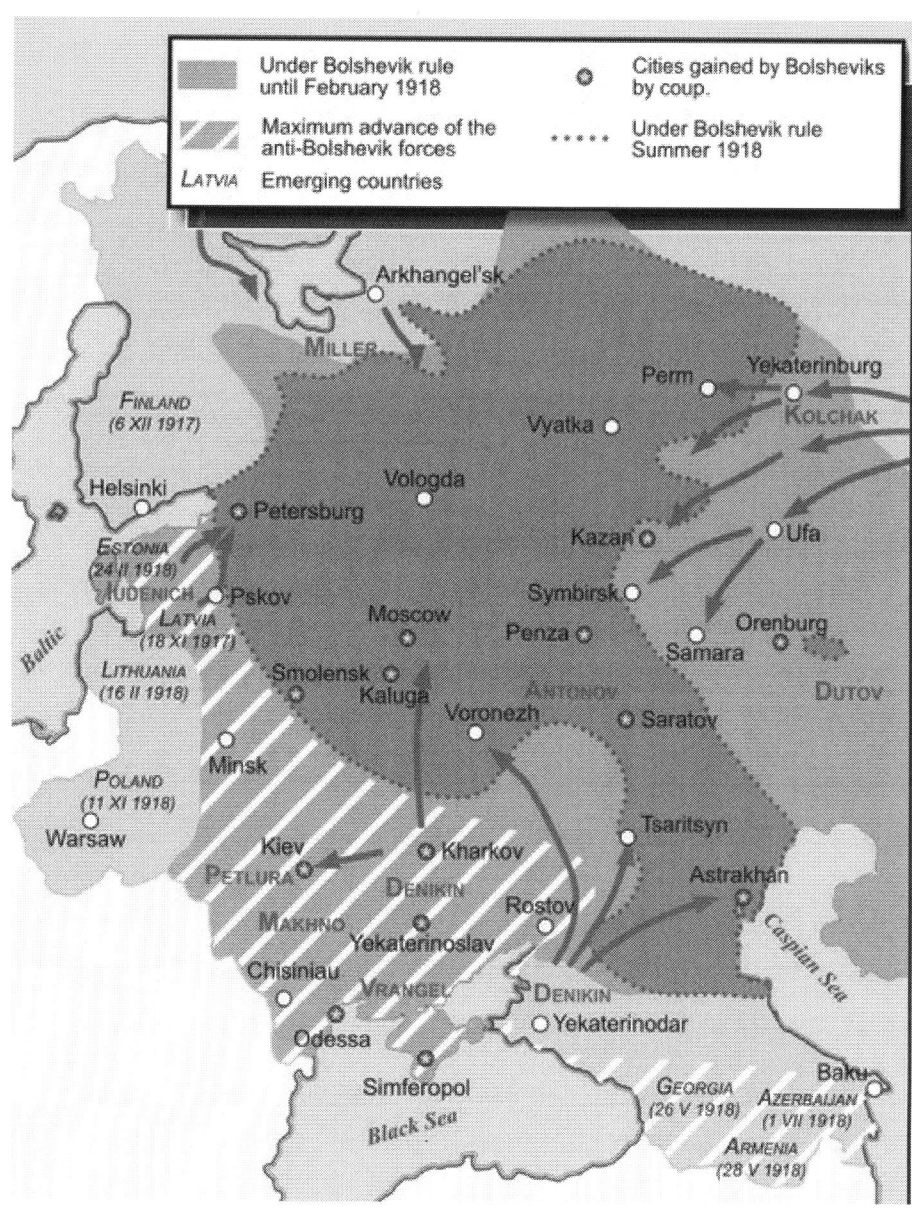

Crimea changed hands several times over the course of the conflict and several political entities were set up on the peninsula. These included:

Crimean People's Republic — December 1917–January 1918 — Crimean Tatar government

Taurida Soviet Socialist Republic — 19 March 1918–30 April 1918 — Bolshevik government

German and Ukrainian People's Republic occupation — May 1918–June 1918

First Crimean Regional Government — 25 June 1918–25 November 1918 — German puppet state under Lipka Tatar General Maciej (Suleyman) Sulkiewicz

Second Crimean Regional Government — November 1918–April 1919 — Anti-Bolshevik government under Crimean Karaite former Kadet member Solomon Krym

Crimean Socialist Soviet Republic — 2 April 1919–June 1919 — Bolshevik government

South Russian Government — February 1920–April 1920 — Government of White movement's General Anton Denikin

Government of South Russia — April 1920 (officially, 16 August 1920)–16 November 1920 — Government of White movement's General Pyotr Wrangel

Bolshevik Revolutionary committee government — November 1920–18 October 1921 — Bolshevik government under Béla Kun (until 20 February 1921), then Mikhail Poliakov

Crimean Autonomous Socialist Soviet Republic — 18 October 1921–30 June 1945 — Autonomous republic of the RSFSR in the Soviet Union

CRIMEA IN THE SOVIET UNION

During the Russian Civil War following the overthrow of the Russian Empire, Crimea changed hands a number of times and was a stronghold of the anti-Bolshevik White Army. It was in Crimea that the White Russians led by General Wrangel made their last stand against the Anarchist forces of Nestor Makhno and the Red Army in 1920. Approximately 50,000 White prisoners of war and civilians were summarily executed by shooting or hanging after the defeat of General Wrangel at the end of 1920. This is considered one of the largest massacres in the Civil War.

With the exception of the pogroms perpetrated in 1919-1921 in the Ukraine and Belarus by most diverse armed units, civilian massacres reached their apogee in Crimea during the evacuation of the White Army's last units. In a matter of weeks (from mid-November to the end of December 1920), approximately 50,000 persons where shot or hung, the majority civilians, often belonging to the social elite, who had followed the White Army's retreat to the Crimean peninsula. Firstly (from mid-November to the beginning of December), massacres of civilians who had not embarked with the troops being evacuated, "spontaneously" multiplied. Secondly, the Bolshevik authorities began registering the population of the main Crimean towns as accurately as possible, given the circumstances. Each inhabitant had to register with the local Cheka by completing a lengthy investigative questionnaire. On the basis of this "investigation" the population was classified in three categories: to be shot, to be sent to concentration camp, to be spared.

On 18 October 1921, the Crimean Autonomous Soviet Socialist Republic (ASSR) was created as part of the Russian SFSR, which then became part of the Soviet Union.

Famine

Crimea experienced two severe famines in the 20th century, the Famine of 1921–1922 and the Holodomor of 1932–1933. A large Slavic population influx occurred in the 1930s as a result of the Soviet policy of regional development. With These demographic changes permanently altered the ethnic balance in the region.

The Holodomor (Ukrainian "Extermination by hunger" was a man-made famine in the Ukrainian Soviet Socialist Republic in 1932 and 1933 that killed up to 7.5 million Ukrainians. During the famine, millions of citizens of Ukrainian SSR, the majority of whom were Ukrainians, died of starvation in a peacetime catastrophe unprecedented in the history of Ukraine.

Early estimates of the death toll by scholars and government officials varied greatly; anywhere from 1.8 to 12 million ethnic Ukrainians were said to have perished as a result of the famine. Recent research has since narrowed the estimates to between 2.4 and 7.5 million. The exact number of deaths is hard to determine, due to a lack of records, but the number increases significantly when the deaths inside heavily Ukrainian-populated Kuban are included. Older estimates are still often cited in political commentary. According to the decision of Kyiv Appellation Court, the demographic losses due to the famine amounted to 10 million, with 3.9 million famine deaths, and a 6.1 million birth deficit.

Scholars disagree on the relative importance of natural factors and bad economic policies as causes of the famine and the degree to which the destruction of the Ukrainian peasantry was premeditated on the part of Joseph Stalin. Using Holodomor in reference to the famine emphasizes its man-made aspects, arguing that actions such as rejection of outside aid, confiscation of all household foodstuffs, and restriction of population movement confer intent, defining the famine as genocide; the loss of life has been compared to the Holocaust. If Soviet policies and actions were conclusively documented as intending to eradicate the rise of Ukrainian nationalism, they would fall under the legal definition of genocide. In the absence of absolute documentary proof of intent, scholars have also made the argument that the Holodomor was ultimately a consequence of the economic problems associated with radical economic changes implemented during the period of liquidation of private property and Soviet industrialization.

Crimean People's Republic

In its founding, the Crimean People's Republic was one of many short-lived attempts to create new states after the Russian Revolution of 1917 had caused the Russian Empire to collapse. It existed from December 1917 to January 1918 in the Crimean Peninsula, south of the present-day Ukraine. The Republic was the first attempt in the Muslim world to establish a state that was secular.

The Crimean People's Republic was declared by the initiative of the Qurultay of Crimean Tatars, which stipulated the equality of all ethnicities within the peninsula; the majority of the people living in the Crimea at the time were Russian (then comprising 42% of the population of the Crimea) or Ukrainian (11%). However the Crimean Tatars were for a while the dominant political and cultural force on the peninsula. Noman Çelebicihan was the first President of the nascent Republic.

The Qurultay consisted of 76 delegates, four of whom were female. The Qurultay in opposition to the Bolsheviks published a *Crimean Tatar Basic Law*, which convened an All-Crimean Constitutional Assembly, established a Board of Directors as a provisional government, and erected a Council of National Representatives as a provisional parliament. The Board of Directors and the Central Council of Ukraine both mutually recognized each other.

1917

December 16

This attempt to build a new nation was quickly defeated by the Bolshevik and anarchist-dominated Black Sea Fleet. Already on December 16, 1917, Bolsheviks had captured Sevastopol where the headquarters of the Black Sea Fleet were located and dissolved the local council of deputies. The power in the city was transferred to the local revkom. The Bolsheviks were supported by some ships of the Black Sea Fleet.

December

To defend itself, the Crimean government created a United Crimean Headquarters that had at its disposal two cavalry and one infantry regiment of Crimean Tatars as well as some Ukrainian and Russian formations that amounted to some thousand people.

1918

January

Several armed incidents took place during January 1918. On January 14, 1918, the Bolsheviks captured Simferopol where they managed to arrest former President of Crimea (Head of Directorate) Noman Çelebicihan who had just resigned on January 4, 1918. He was transferred back to Sevastopol and interned until February 23, 1918, when he was shot without trial. The body of Çelebicihan was thrown into the sea.

On the initiative of Çelebicihan on January 10, 1918, the Qurultay created a special commission that conducted talks with the Bolsheviks to stop the armed conflict in Crimea.

By the end of January 1918 the Bolsheviks had captured the whole of Crimea and dissolved both the Qurultay as well as the Council of National Representatives. A mass terror engulfed the peninsula based on class struggle and ethnic cleansing. With Çelebicihan in the Reds' custody, another leader of the Crimean Tatars, Jafer Seidamet, managed to escape to the Caucasus across continental Ukraine. Many Crimean military formations retreated to the mountains. The government of Ukraine blockaded Crimea, while trying to reestablish control over the Black Sea Fleet and the city of Sevastopol. Any Muslim supporting military formations on the way to Crimea was stopped. That in turn triggered a protest from the All-Russian Muslim military *suro* (council). By the end of January 1918, the Ukrainian government itself was forced to declare war on the Russian SFSR due to advancement of the Red Guard forces of Moscow and Petrograd into Ukraine without explicit notification.

Taurida Soviet Socialist Republic

The Crimean People's Republic had been overrun by Bolshevik forces. In Simferopol *a guberniya revkom* was established which possessed sufficient authority as the military center continued to be located in Sevastopol.

February 10–12

To liquidate this dual authority there took place a conference of *revkoms* at which participated 44 delegates (including 27 Bolsheviks). The conference was later recognized as an extraordinary congress of the Soviets of Workers and Soldiers Deputies. At the meeting it was decided to create 14 commissariats. The congress also confirmed the disbandment of the Council of People's Representatives and *Qurultay.* The local administration was transformed into a system of soviets replacing the old system of duma and land administration *(zemstvo)*. The 14-member Central Executive Committee was established as the central administration of *guberniya* which consisted of 10 Bolsheviks; the rest were Left SRs. Zh.Miller (Bolshevik) was appointed as chairman of the committee.

The congress, with 23 votes "for" and 20 "against", decided that the administrative center would be in Simferopol rather than Sevastopol, while the military center, which was subordinated to the central executive committee, was left in Sevastopol. The major administrative and political issues were to be decided by laws adopted at the 3rd All-Russian Congress of Soviets. The Taurida congress also approved the adoption of drastic measures for grain procurement allowing requisition and the use of armed force sending bread to industrial areas and the army.

Establishment of the Soviet Autonomous Republic

March 19 and 21

A few weeks later, decrees of the Taurida Central Executive Committee (CEC) issued in Simferopol established the Taurida Soviet Socialist Republic on the same territory. Areas of Taurida that lay north of Crimea were also claimed by the Donetsk-Krivoy Rog Soviet Republic and the Ukrainian People's Republic.

With the assistance of the German Empire, the Taurida Soviet Socialist Republic was quickly overrun by forces of the Ukrainian People's Republic during the Crimean Offensive.

end of April

The majority of the CEC and the Council of People's Commissars, including council leader Anton Słucki and local Bolshevik chief Jan Tarwacki, were arrested and shot in Alushta by German troops. On 30 April, the Republic was abolished.

Aftermath

Following the invasion, a German-protected Crimean Regional Government was established under Maciej Sulkiewicz and, later, Solomon Krym. After the defeat of the White Movement's Volunteer Army and the reassertion of Soviet control in late 1920, the lands of the former Republic were divided between the peninsular Crimean Autonomous Soviet Socialist Republic under the Russian SFSR and the mainland Ukrainian SSR. Currently, the entire area is part of Ukraine.

The Bolsheviks briefly established the Taurida Soviet Socialist Republic on Crimean territory in early 1918 before the area was overrun by forces of the Ukrainian People's Republic and the German Empire. Some officials of the

National government such as Cafer Seydahmet Kırımer who managed to escape the Bolsheviks' terror sought political asylum in Kiev and petitioned for military help from the advancing Ukrainian Army as well as the forces of the Central powers.

Crimean Autonomous Soviet Socialist Republic

1921

October 18

The Crimean Autonomous Soviet Socialist Republic was created as part of the Russian SFSR which, in turn, became part of the new Soviet Union. However, this did not protect the Crimean Tatars (who then constituted about 25% of the Crimean population) from Joseph Stalin's repressions of the 1930s. The Greeks were another cultural group that suffered. Their lands were lost during the process of collectivisation, in which farmers were not compensated with wages. Schools which taught Greek were closed and Greek literature was destroyed, because the Soviets considered the Greeks as counter-revolutionary with their links to the capitalist state of Greece, and their independent culture.

1930's Ukraine and Crimea under Stalin

In 1927, Stalin emerged as the new leader of the USSR from the power struggle, which took place within the Communist Party after Lenin's death.

In 1928 the first five-year plan for economic changes was accepted. It was based on the projects of industrialisation, urbanisation and collectivisation.

Industrialisation

Out of 1500 new facilities built in the USSR, 400 were located in Ukraine. Among them were Dniproges (the biggest hydroelectric power plant in Europe built in 1932), the metallurgic plant in Zaporozhie and the tractor plant in Kharkov. The facilities built during the first five-year plan placed Ukraine among the leading industrial countries of Europe.[28] However, such progress called for the involvement of thousands of workers. To cultivate motivation and enthusiasm, different methods were used. On one hand, the best workers were publicly praised and honoured. On the other hand, being late to or absent from work was considered a criminal offence, which led to punishment.

Urbanisation

Another feature of the 1930s was rapid urbanisation. Thousands of workers moved from the rural areas to the cities to work for the developing industry. Andrei K. Sokolov indicates that "between 1926 and 1939 the country's urban population increased from 18 to 33 per cent".

Collectivisation

The changes in the rural areas were also drastic. Collectivisation (creating collective farms from private ones) was defined by historian Orest Subtelny as "one of the most terrible events in the history of Ukraine". Peasants' support for collectivisation was absent and Stalin realised that to achieve his aims both economic and political control had to be enforced. First of all he initiated a campaign against the rich peasants (kurkuls) calling for their elimination as a social class. In practice this meant executions, deportations to the labour camps in Siberia or confiscation of all the kurkuls' property.

However, not only rich peasants opposed collectivisation. Peasants expressed their discontent by organising armed revolts or killing their own cattle just to prevent the authorities from having it. Consequently, in 1928-1929 the number of livestock in Ukraine halved.

Holodomor

The famine of 1932-1933 (Holodomor) became one of the most tragic events in the history of Ukraine. While the exact number of lives claimed by the famine is unknown, it is thought to range from 5 to 10 million.[34] The harvest of 1932 was only 12 per cent less than the average of 1926-1930. However, the authorities continued with the systematic confiscation of grain from peasants while Stalin upped the grain quota by 44 per cent.[35] Death or ten years at labour camps was announced as a punishment for those who did not contribute to the state's grain collection. Robert Conquest notes that even though there is no direct proof that the famine was planned by Stalin beforehand, his policies show that he considered it as an effective way to punish Ukrainian peasantry for their resistance to collectivisation and the existence of the 'kurkul-nationalist element'.

A special law was passed in Moscow prohibiting the distribution of grain to peasants before the state plan was fully executed. Special commissions were searching for grain and even those who were dying of hunger were not allowed to keep anything. According to Subtelny, peasants had to resort to eating cats, dogs, rats, leaves, and even cases of cannibalism were not uncommon. Nevertheless, while the villages were dying of hunger, the party activists kept collecting grain.

Soviet authorities attempted to cover up the events of 1932-33, denying the occurrence of the famine till the last days of the Soviet Union. Only after Ukraine became an independent state was the Holodomor famine admitted. In 2006 the Ukrainian parliament accepted the "About Holodomor in Ukraine in 1932-1933" law, which defined the famine as genocide against the Ukrainian nation. Even though it is still disputable among historians whether or not one can define it as genocide, 26 countries have recognised Holodomor as such.

The Great Terror

The 1930s are known in the Soviet history as the time of Great Terror. Ukraine suffered heavily under Soviet mass repressions. In 1929-1930 45 leading scientists, scholars and writers were arrested for belonging to the fictitious "Union for Ukraine's Liberation". This fake organisation invented by the Soviet authorities was declared to be aiming for Stalin's assassination and the separation of Ukraine from the USSR.

In 1933, repressions against Ukrainian party members started. They were excluded from the party for "ideological mistakes" which in reality amounted to open or potential disagreement with Stalin's policies.[39] Those who spearheaded the "Ukrainisation" policy in the 1920s were accused of supporting "cultural counterrevolution" and "isolating Ukrainian workers from the beneficial influence of Russian culture". Thousands of members of the new Soviet intelligentsia were sent to labour camps or executed; out of 240 Ukrainian writers, 200 disappeared. Out of 85 linguists, 62 were killed.

The terror was widespread. Suspicion and fear became the reality of the time. In 1937 Stalin decided to eliminate the Ukrainian Communist Party's leadership as well as the Ukrainian Soviet government. Three Stalin's representatives - Vyacheslav Molotov, Nikolay Yezhov and Nikita Khrushchev - were sent to Kiev to carry out the 'purge'. By June 1938, 17 ministers of the Ukrainian government and almost all members of the Central Committee had been arrested and executed. Overall, the repressions affected 37 per cent of Ukrainian Communist Party members, i.e. about 170 000 people. "It can seem a paradox that they were executing their 'own men' – the leading activists of the party and state, famous military commanders," notes Zaitsev and explains that:

...there was nothing strange about it because "old activists" who had survived conspiracy and tsarist repressions, civil war and believed in the ideals of the revolution were not fit for the ruling class, whilst being "fathers of nation" at the top of the bureaucratic pyramid. They had to be eliminated to assign the new bureaucracy that entered the party after the revolution and did not have old-fashioned revolutionary fantasies and would be faithful to the leader.

World War II

The Yalta Conference,

Sometimes called the Crimea Conference and codenamed the Argonaut Conference, held February 4–11, 1945, this was the World War II meeting of the heads of government of the United States, the United Kingdom and the Soviet Union (represented by President Franklin D. Roosevelt, Prime Minister Winston Churchill and Premier Joseph Stalin) to discuss Europe's post-war reorganization. The conference convened in the Livadia Palace near Yalta in Crimea.

The meeting was intended mainly to discuss the re-establishment of the nations of wartorn Europe. Within a few years, with the Cold War dividing the continent, Yalta became a subject of intense controversy, and to some extent, it has remained controversial.

Yalta was the second of three wartime conferences among the Big Three. It had been preceded by the Tehran Conference in 1943, and was followed by the Potsdam Conference in July 1945, which was attended by Stalin, Churchill and Harry S Truman, who had replaced the late President Roosevelt.

The Crimea Campaign

An eight-month long campaign by Axis forces to conquer the Crimea peninsula was the scene of some of the bloodiest battles on the Eastern Front during World War II. The German, Romanian, and defending Soviet troops suffered heavy casualties as the Axis forces tried to advance through the Isthmus of Perekop linking the Crimean peninsula to the mainland at Perekop, from summer of 1941 through to the first half of 1942.

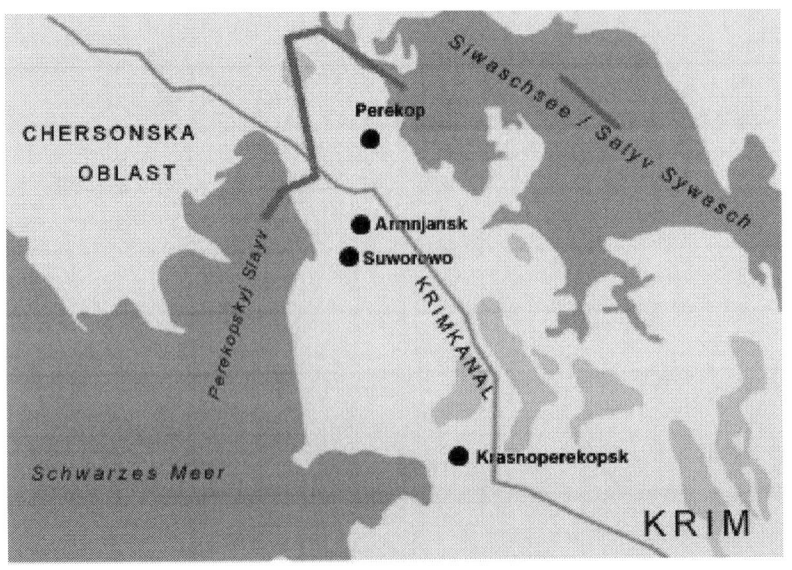

From the 26 September 1941 the German and Romanian Armies were involved in the fighting, opposed by the Red Army and elements of the Black Sea Fleet. Once the German and Romanian troops broke through, they occupied most of Crimea, with the exception of the city of Sevastopol, which was given the title of Hero City for its resistance, and Kerch, which was recaptured by the Soviets during an amphibious operation near the end of 1941 and then taken once again by the Germans during Operation Bustard Hunt on 8 May.

Battle of the Kerch Peninsula

26 December 1941 — 19 May 1942 (4 months, and 23 days)

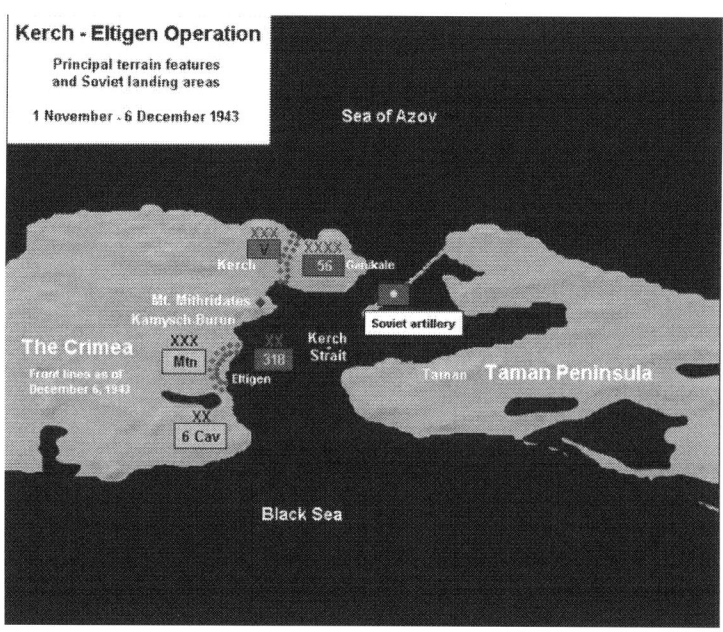

On 26 December 1941, the Soviets landed on Kerch, and on 30 December executed another landing near Feodosiya. The operation was to drive to Sevastopol and relieve the garrison, now encircled by the German Army. The Soviets consolidated their bridgeheads and defeated the attacking Romanian brigades. German General Manstein diverted his troops from Sevastopol and succeeded in sealing off the Soviet armies in the Kerch peninsula. But the Soviet landings had saved Sevastopol and seized the initiative. Casualties were high. The Germans lost 8,595 between 17 and 31 December. The Soviets lost 7,000 killed and another 20,000 as prisoners of war.

But later, the Germans using overwhelming air and ground forces over 12 days, Kerch finally fell. Some 116,045 Soviet soldiers were evacuated by sea. However, 162,282 were left behind, killed or captured. The Germans claimed to have taken 170,000 prisoners, but this number included a large number of civilians. German casualties amounted to only 3,397 casualties including 600 dead.

The Siege of Sevastopol

The Siege of Sevastopol lasted 250 days from 30 October 1941 until 4 July 1942, when the Axis finally captured the city. The campaign was fought by the Axis powers of Germany, Romania, and Italy against the Soviet Union for control of Sevastopol, a port in the Crimea on the Black Sea. On 22 June 1941 the Axis invaded the Soviet Union during Operation Barbarossa. Axis land forces reached the Crimea in the autumn of 1941 and overran most of the area. The only objective not in Axis hands was Sevastopol. Several attempts were made to secure the city in October and November 1941. A major attack was planned for late November, but heavy rains delayed the Axis attack until 17 December 1941. Under the command of Erich von Manstein, Axis forces were unable to capture Sevastopol during this first operation. Soviet forces launched an amphibious landing on the Crimean peninsula at Kerch in December 1941 to relieve the siege and force the Axis to divert forces to defend their gains. The operation saved Sevastopol for the time being, but the bridgehead in the eastern Crimea was eliminated in May 1942.

After the failure of their first assault on Sevastopol, the Axis opted to conduct siege warfare until the middle of 1942, at which point they attacked the encircled Soviet forces by land, sea, and air. On 2 June 1942, the Axis began this operation, codenamed *Sturgeon Catch*. The Soviet Red Army and Black Sea Fleet held out for weeks under intense Axis bombardment. The German Air Force played a vital part in the siege. The Luftwaffe made up for a shortage of Axis artillery, providing highly effective aerial bombardment in support of the ground forces. Finally, on 4 July 1942, the remaining Soviet forces surrendered and the Axis seized the port. Both sides had suffered considerable losses during the siege and attack.

The Germans claimed that over 90,000 Red Army soldiers had been taken prisoner, and an even greater number killed. However, this claim appears to be overstated as, according to Soviet sources, the Soviet garrison defending Sevastopol totaled 106,000 men beforehand (and received only 3,000 reinforcements during the attack), while it is known that 25,157 persons were evacuated, the overwhelming majority being either wounded soldiers or officers evacuated on Stalin's orders.

In 1944, Sevastopol came under the control of troops from the Soviet Union. The so-called "City of Russian Glory" once known for its beautiful architecture was entirely destroyed and had to be rebuilt stone by stone. Due to its enormous historical and symbolic meaning for the Russians, it became a priority for Stalin and the Soviet government to have it restored to its former glory within the shortest time possible.

Deportation of the Crimean Tatars

Sürgünlik (Crimean Tatar for "exile") refers to the state-organized and forcible deportation of the Crimean Tatars from the Crimean Peninsula by the Soviet Union in 1944. The Tatars were mostly deported to the Uzbek SSR. Advocacy groups against the process use a steam engine as a symbol, making reference to the cattle trains used in the deportation.

In 1944, the Crimea was recaptured by troops of the 4th Ukrainian Front during the Crimean Offensive (8 April 1944 – 12 May 1944), under the false pretext of alleged collaboration between the Crimean Tatars and the Nazis during the Nazi occupation of the Crimea in 1941–1944, the Soviet government evicted the Crimean Tatar people from Crimea on orders of Joseph Stalin and Lavrentiy Beria.

Only 9,225 Crimean Tatars served in anti-Soviet Tatar Legions and other German formed battalions.

The deportation began on 18 May 1944 in all Crimean inhabited localities. More than 32,000 NKVD troops participated in this action. The forced deportees were given only 30 minutes to gather personal belongings, after which they were loaded onto cattle trains and moved out of Crimea. 193,865 Crimean Tatars were deported, 151,136 of them to Uzbek SSR, 8,597 to Mari ASSR, 4,286 to Kazakh SSR, the rest 29,846 to the various oblasts of Russian SFSR. At the same moment, most of the Crimean Tatar men who were fighting in the ranks of the Red Army were demobilized and sent into forced labor camps in Siberia and in the Ural mountain region.

The deportation was poorly planned and executed; local authorities in the destination areas were not properly informed about the scale of the matter and did not receive enough resources to accommodate the deportees. The lack of accommodation and food, the failure to adapt to new climatic conditions and the rapid spread of diseases had a heavy demographic impact during the first years of exile.

From May to November 10,105 Crimean Tatars died of starvation in Uzbekistan (7% of those deported to the Uzbek SSR). Nearly 30,000 (20%) died in exile during the year and a half by the NKVD data. Due to hunger, thirst and disease, around 45% of the total population died in the process of deportation. According to Soviet dissident information, many Crimean Tatars were made to work in the large-scale projects conducted by the Soviet GULAG system. Crimean Tatar activists tried to evaluate the demographic consequences of the deportation. They carried out a census in all the scattered Tatar communities in the middle of the 1960s. The results of this inquiry show that 109,956 (46.2%) Crimean Tatars of the 238,500 deportees died between July 1, 1944 and January 1, 1947.

Crimean activists call for the recognition of the Sürgünlik as genocide. The Crimean Tatar population experienced a significant decline in Crimea during exile and were displaced as a majority by ethnic Russians.

Return to Crimea

By the end of summer 1944, the ethnic cleansing of Crimea was complete. In 1967, the Crimean Tatars were rehabilitated, but they were banned from legally returning to their homeland until the last days of the Soviet Union.

Although a 1967 Soviet decree removed the charges against Crimean Tatars, the Soviet government did nothing to facilitate their resettlement in Crimea and to make reparations for lost lives and confiscated property. Crimean Tatars, having definite tradition of non-communist political dissent, succeeded in creating a truly independent network of activists, values and political experience. Crimean Tatars, led by Crimean Tatar National Movement Organization, were not allowed to return to Crimea from exile until the beginning of the Perestroika in the mid-1980s.

On March 11, 2014 the Crimean parliament recognized the deportation of Crimean Tatars as a tragic fate.

1945, June 30

The *Crimean ASSR* was converted into the *Crimean Oblast of the RSFSR* on by the decree of the both presidiums of the Supreme Soviet of USSR and the Supreme Soviet of RSFSR

1954, February 19

The oblast was then transferred from the Russian SFSR to the Ukrainian SSR within the Soviet Union; its capital was the city of Simferopol. The Crimean Oblast, at that time was desertic and without infrastructures, it was transferred to the Ukrainian SSR as a "symbolic gesture" marking the 300th anniversary of Ukraine becoming a part of the Russian Empire. This Supreme Soviet Decree states that this transfer was motivated by *the commonality of the economy, the proximity, and close economic and cultural relations between the Crimean region and the Ukrainian SSR*. The General Secretary of the Communist Party in Soviet Union at the time was Ukrainian native Nikita Khrushchev.

A significant part of the ASSR's prewar population were Crimean Tatars, who were stripped of their property and civil rights and forcibly resettled to Central Asia in 1944. The constitutional rights of the Tatars were restored with a decree dated September 5, 1967, but they were not allowed to return until the last days of the Soviet Union.

In post-war years, Crimea thrived as a tourist destination, with new attractions and sanatoriums for tourists. Tourists came from all around the Soviet Union and neighbouring countries, particularly from the German Democratic Republic. In time the peninsula also became a major tourist destination for cruises originating in Greece and Turkey. Crimea's infrastructure and manufacturing also developed, particularly around the sea ports at Kerch and Sevastopol and in the oblast's landlocked capital, Simferopol. Populations of Ukrainians and Russians alike doubled, with more than 1.6 million Russians and 626,000 Ukrainians living on the peninsula by 1989.

1991, January 20

Following a referendum, the Crimean Oblast was upgraded to that of an *Autonomous Soviet Socialist Republic* on February 12, 1991, by the Supreme Soviet of the Ukrainian SSR

Crimea within independent Ukraine

With the collapse of the Soviet Union, Crimea became part of the newly independent Ukraine. Independence was supported by a referendum in all regions of Ukrainian SSR, including Crimea. 54% of the Crimean voters supported independence with a 60% turnout (in Sevastopol 57% supported independence).The percentage of the total Crimean electorate that had voted for Ukrainian independence in the referendum was 37%. In 1994, the legal status of Crimea as part of Ukraine was backed up by Russia, who pledged to uphold the territorial integrity of Ukraine in a memorandum signed in 1994, also signed by the US, UK and France.

With the collapse of the Soviet Union, Crimea became part of the newly independent Ukraine, which led to tensions between Russia and Ukraine. With the Russian Black Sea Fleet based on the peninsula, worries of armed skirmishes were occasionally raised. Crimean Tatars began returning from exile and resettling in Crimea.

August 24

Yuriy Meshkov established the Republican Movement of Crimea.

Following a failed Communist Party-led coup attempt against Soviet leader Mikhail Gorbachev, Ukraine declared its independence.

September 2

The National Movement of Crimean Tatars appealed to the Extraordinary Congress of People's Deputies in Russia demanding a program for return of the deported Tatar population back to Crimea.

December 5

In December of that year, with the final dissolution of the Soviet Union, Ukraine was recognized as one of 12 countries — acknowledged now as the Commonwealth of Independent States — that once comprised the core of the Soviet Union.

Into democracy: Ukraine elects its first ever president, Leonid Kravchuk. Plagued by economic problems, Kravchuk fails to win re-election in 1994 against his former prime minister, Leonid Kuchma.

1992

February 26

The Verkhovniy Sovet (the Crimean parliament) renamed the ASSR the *Republic of Crimea*

May 5, 6

Verkhovniy Sovet proclaimed self-government and passed the first Crimean constitution the same day. On 6 May 1992 the same parliament inserted a new sentence into this constitution that declared that Crimea was part of Ukraine.

May 19

Crimea agreed to remain as part of Ukraine and annulled their proclamation of self-government.

June 30

Crimean Communists forced the Kiev government to expand on the already extensive autonomous status of Crimea. In the same period, Russian president Boris Yeltsin and Ukraine's Leonid Kravchuk agreed to divide the former Soviet Black Sea Fleet between Russia and the newly formed Ukrainian Navy.

October 24

Meshkov re-registered his movement as the Republican Party of Crimea

December 11

The President of Ukraine called the attempt of the Russian deputies to charge the Russian parliament with a task to define the status of Sevastopol as an imperial disease.

December 17

The office of The Ukrainian Presidential Representative In Crimea was created.

1993

January 10

Creation of the office of The Ukrainian Presidential Representative caused a wave of protests and an unsanctioned rally by the Sevastopol branches of the National Salvation Front, the Russian Popular Assembly, and the All-Crimean Movement of the Voters for the Republic of Crimea. The protest was held in Sevastopol at Nakhimov Square

January 15

Kravchuk and Yeltsin in the meeting in Moscow appointed Eduard Baltin as the commander of the Black Sea Fleet. At the same time the Union of the Ukrainian Naval Officers protested the Russian intervention into the Ukrainian internal affairs. Soon after that there were more anti-Ukrainian protests led by the Meshkov's party, the Voters for the Crimean Republic, Yedinstvo, and the Union of Communists that demanded to turn Sevastopol under the Russian jurisdiction and followed by the interview given by the Sevastopol's Communist, Vasyl Parkhomenko, who said that the city's Communists request to recognize the Russian as the state language and restoration of the Soviet Union.

March 19

Alexander Kruglov, Crimean deputy and the member of the National Salvation Front, threatened the members of the Crimean Ukrainian Congress not allow into the building of the Republican Council. Couple of days after that Russia established an information center in Sevastopol.

April

The Ukrainian Ministry of Defence submitted an appeal to Verkhovna Rada to suspend the Yalta Agreement of 1992 that divided the Black Sea Fleet that was followed by the request from the Ukrainian Republican Party to recognize the Fleet either fully Ukrainian or a fleet of a foreign country in Ukraine. Also over 300 Russian legislators called the planned Congress of Ukrainian Residents a political provocation.

On 14 April the Presidium of the Crimean parliament called for the creation of the presidential post of the Crimean Republic. A week later the Russian deputy, Valentin Agafonov, stated that Russia is ready to supervise the referendum on Crimean independence and include the republic as a separate entity in the CIS.

July 28

Viktor Prusakov, one of the leaders of the Russian Society of Crimea, , stated that his organization is ready for an armed mutiny and establishment of the Russian administration in Sevastopol.

September

Eduard Baltin accused Ukraine of converting some of his fleet and conducting an armed assault on his personnel, and threatened to take countermeasures of placing the fleet on alert.

October 14

The Crimean parliament established the post of President of Crimea and agreed on the quota of the Crimean Tatars representation in the Council to 14. The head of the Russian People's Council in Sevastopol, Alexander Kruglov, called it excessive. The chairman of the Tatar Mejlis, Mustafa Abdülcemil Qırımoğlu, used words "categorically against" in regards to the proposed election for Crimean president on 16 January. He stated that there cannot be two presidents in a single state.

November 6

Yuriy Osmanov, the Crimean Tatar leader, was murdered. Series of terrorist actions rocked the peninsula in the winter among them were the arson of the Mejlis apartment, the shooting of a Ukrainian official, several hooligan attacks on Meshkov, the bomb explosion in the house of a local parliamentary, the assassination attempt on a Communist presidential candidate, and others.

1994

January 2

The Mejlis announced a boycott of the presidential elections, which were later canceled. The boycott itself was later taken on by other Crimean Tatar organizations.

January 11, 12

The Mejlis announced their representative, Mykola Bahrov, the speaker of the Crimean parliament, as the presidential candidate. Some other candidates accused Bahrov of severe methods of agitation. At the same time, Vladimir Zhirinovsky called on the people of Crimea to vote for the Russian Sergei Shuvainikov.

January 30

The pro-Russian Yuriy Meshkov was elected to the new post but quickly ran into conflicts with parliament.

September 8

The Crimean parliament degraded the President's powers from the Head Of State to the Head Of The Executive power only, to which Meshkov responded by disbanding parliament and announcing his control over Crimea four days later. Amendments to the constitution eased the conflict[citation needed],

1995

March 17

The parliament of Ukraine intervened, scrapping the Crimean Constitution and removing Meshkov along with his office for his actions against the state and promoting integration with Russia.

1996

April 4

An interim constitution was put into effect and lasted from 4 April 1996 to 23 December 1998, when a new constitution was accepted, changing the territory's name to the *Autonomous Republic of Crimea*.

1997

May 31

In the first visit from Moscow since the Soviet collapse, Russian President Boris Yeltsin (left) and Ukrainian President Leonid Kuchma signed the Treaty of Friendship, Cooperation and Partnership in Kiev, marking a rapprochement of a history fraught with painful ties.

Following the ratification of the Treaty of Friendship, Cooperation, and Partnership on friendship and division of the Black Sea Fleet, international tensions slowly eased. With the treaty, Moscow recognized Ukraine's borders and territorial integrity, and accepted Ukraine's sovereignty over Crimea and Sevastopol. In a separate agreement, Russia was to receive 80 percent of the Black Sea Fleet and use of the military facilities in Sevastopol on a 20-year lease.

However, other controversies between Ukraine and Russia still remain, including the ownership of a lighthouse on Cape Sarych. Because the Russian Navy controlled 77 geographical objects on the south Crimean Shore, the Sevastopol Government Court ordered the vacating of the objects, which the Russian military did not carry out.

2004

November- December: The Orange Revolution

The "Orange Revolution" was a series of protests and political events that took place in Ukraine from late November 2004 to January 2005, in the immediate aftermath of the run-off vote of the 2004 Ukrainian presidential election which was claimed to be marred by massive corruption, voter intimidation and direct electoral fraud. Kiev, the Ukrainian capital, was the focal point of the movement's campaign of civil resistance, with thousands of protesters demonstrating daily. Nationwide, the democratic revolution was highlighted by a series of acts of civil disobedience, sit-ins, and general strikes organized by the opposition movement.

The protests were prompted by reports from several domestic and foreign election monitors as well as the widespread public perception that the results of the run-off vote of 21 November 2004 between leading candidates Viktor Yushchenko and Viktor Yanukovych were rigged by the authorities in favour of Yanukovych. The nationwide protests succeeded when the results of the original run-off were annulled, and a revote was ordered by Ukraine's Supreme Court for 26 December 2004. Under intense scrutiny by domestic and international observers, the second run-off was declared to be fair and free. The final results showed a clear victory for Yushchenko, who received about 52% of the vote, compared to Yanukovych's 44%. Yushchenko was declared the official winner and with his inauguration on 23 January 2005 in Kiev, the Orange Revolution ended.

Before his election as President, Yushchenko already had a career in Ukrainian politics. In 1993, he became Governor (head) of the National Bank of Ukraine. From 1998 to 2001 he was Prime Minister. After his dismissal as Prime Minister, Yushchenko went into opposition to President Leonid Kuchma and he founded the Our Ukraine bloc, which at the 2002 parliamentary election became Ukraine's most popular political force, with 23.57% of the votes.

Following an assassination attempt in late 2004 during his election campaign, Yushchenko was confirmed to have ingested hazardous amounts of potent dioxin (a contaminant in Agent Orange). He suffered disfigurement as a result of the poisoning.

Viktor Yuschenko before and after disfigurement

As an informal leader of the Ukrainian opposition coalition, Viktor Andriyovych Yushchenko was one of the two main candidates in the October–November 2004 Ukrainian presidential election. Yushchenko won the presidency through a repeat runoff election between him and Prime Minister Viktor Yanukovych. The Ukrainian Supreme Court called for the runoff election to be repeated because of widespread electoral fraud in favor of Viktor Yanukovych in the original vote. Yushchenko won in the revote (52% to 44%), thus Yushchenko the third president since Ukraine's independence..

Viktor Yanukovitch

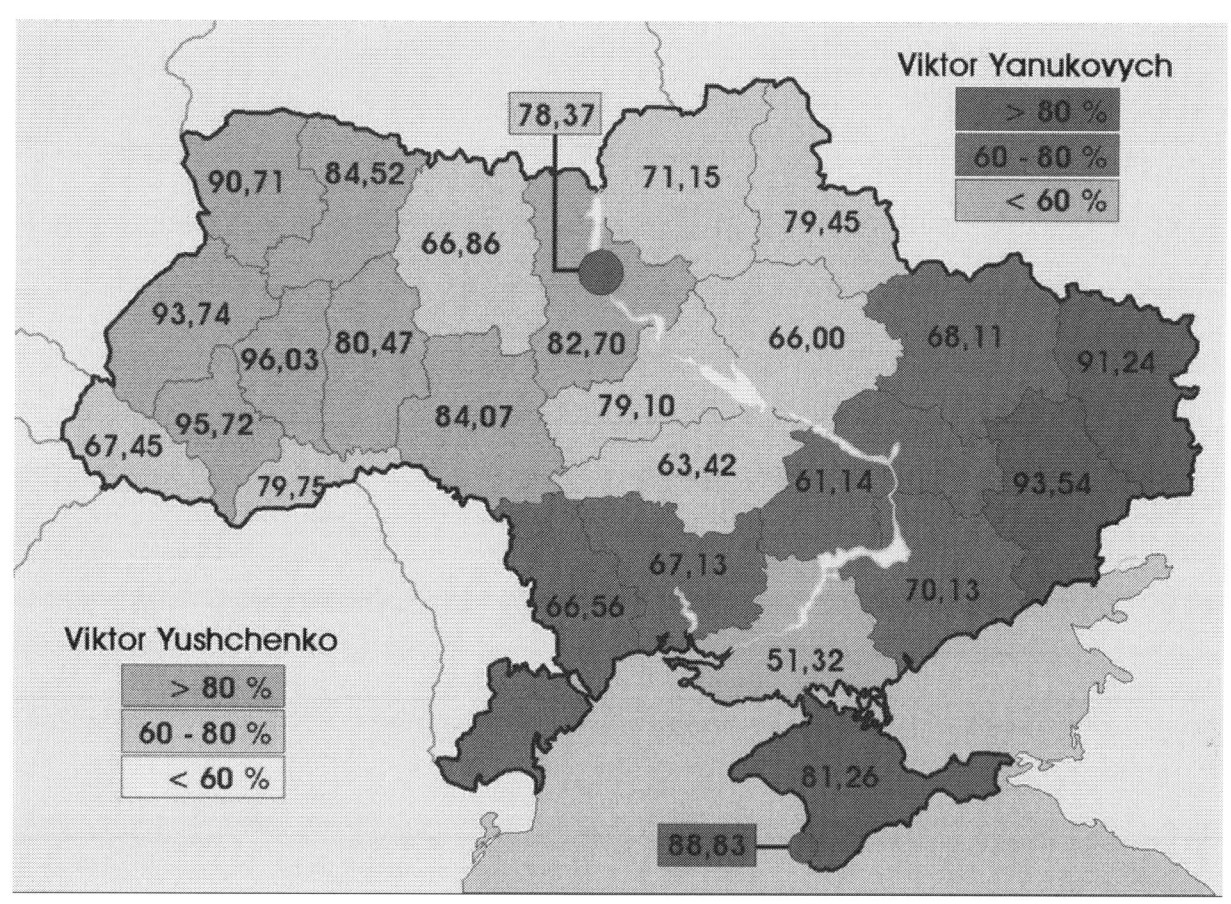

Public protests prompted by the electoral fraud played a major role in that presidential election and led to Ukraine's Orange Revolution.

Orange flags of the Orange Revolution

2005

August 3

The Cape Sarych lighthouse has been controlled by the Russian Army. Through the years, there have been various attempts to return Cape Sarych to Ukrainian territory, all of which were unsuccessful.

2006

Anti-NATO protests broke out on the peninsula after U.S. Marines arrived at the Crimean city of Feodosiya to take part in the *Sea Breeze 2006* Ukraine-NATO military exercise. Protesters greeted the marines with barricades and slogans bearing "Occupiers go home!" and a couple of days later, the Crimean parliament declared Crimea a NATO-free territory. After several days of protest, the U.S. Marines withdrew from the peninsula.

2008

September

The Ukrainian Foreign Minister Volodymyr Ohryzko accused Russia of giving out Russian passports to the population in the Crimea and described it as a "real problem" given Russia's declared policy of military intervention abroad to protect Russian citizens.

2009

January

The SBU started criminal proceedings against the pro-Russian association *People's front Sevastopol-Crimea-Russia*.

February 16

The Mayor of Sevastopol at a press conference in Moscow, citing recent polls, claimed the population of Crimea is opposed to the idea of becoming a part of Russia.

February 17

Although western newspapers like the Wall Street Journal have speculated about a Russian coup in Sevastopol or another Crimean city in connection with the Russian-Georgian war and the Recognition of Abkhazia and South Ossetia by Russia, Valentyn Nalyvaychenko, acting head of the Security Service of Ukraine (SBU), stated that he is confident that any "Ossetian scenario" is impossible in Crimea.

February 19

On the 55th anniversary of the transfer of Crimea transfer of the Russian SFSR to the Ukrainian SSR, some 300 to 500 people took part in rallies to protest against the transfer.

August 24

Anti-Ukrainian demonstrations were held in Crimea by ethnic Russian residents. Sergei Tsekov of the Russian Bloc and then deputy speaker of the Crimean parliament, said he hoped that Russia would treat the Crimea the same way as it had treated South Ossetia and Abkhazia.

2010

February

Yushchenko failed to secure a run-off spot during the 2010 Ukrainian presidential election; gaining 5.5% of the vote. Pro-Russian politician Viktor Yanukovich wins the 2010 presidential election, thus Yanukovych became Yushchenko's successor as Ukrainian President after the Central Election Commission and international observers declared the presidential election were fairly conducted.

Prime Minister Yulia Tymoshenko, who had been a prominent leader of the Orange Revolution, condemns the results as fraudulent. Tymoshenko finally resigns after a no-confidence vote from parliament and the dismissal of her government.

Yanukovych was ousted from power four years later, however, following the February 2014 Euromaidan clashes in Kiev's Independence Square. Unlike the bloodless Orange Revolution, these protests resulted in more than 100 deaths, occurring mostly between February 18 and 20th.

April 27

Chaos in the Ukrainian parliament erupted during a debate over the extension of the lease on a Russian naval base after Ukraine's parliament ratified the treaty that extends Russia's lease on naval moorings and shore installations in port of Sevastopol and other locations in Crimea until 2042 with optional five-year renewals. The Chairman of the Verkhovna Rada, Volodymyr Lytvyn, had to be shielded by umbrellas as he was pelted with eggs, while smoke bombs exploded and politicians brawled. Along with Verkhovna Rada, the treaty was ratified by the Russian State Duma.

2011

August 5

Former Prime Minister Yulia Tymoshenko is arrested on charges of abuse of power by allegedly ordering Naftogaz to sign a disadvantegous gas deal with Russia in 2009. Tymoshenko denies the charges, claiming the arrest is a ploy to keep her from running in any new elections. A court finds Tymoshenko guilty, sentencing her to seven years in prison.

2012

During the 2012 Ukrainian parliamentary elections, Yushchenko headed the election list of *Our Ukraine*. The party won 1.11% of the national votes and no constituencies, and thus failed to win parliamentary representation.

THE CURRENT CRISIS

2013

November 21

Ukraine abruptly abandons a proposed trade pact with the European Union. Instead, Ukrainian President Viktor Yanukovich announces closer ties to Russia, which is accused of strong-arming Ukraine by threatening to cut energy supplies.

November 24

The government decision to abandon the EU agreement sees tens of thousands of demonstrators flood the streets, creating the largest protest in Ukraine since the 2004 Orange Revolution.

December 1

The number of protesters swells to roughly 350,000, and some begin to turn violent, as a group of demonstrators besiege the president's office. Demonstrators also occupy Kiev's city hall.

December 8

Protesters destroy the last statue of Vladimir Lenin in Kiev as protesters sing the Ukrainian national anthem and take pieces of the rubble as souvenirs.

December 17

Russia signs a deal with Ukraine intended to help Ukraine stave off economic crisis. In the pact, Russia agrees to buy $15 billion of Ukrainian bonds and reduce the price of Russian gas destined for Ukraine by one-third.

2014

January 17

President Viktor Yanukovich signs an anti-protest law that introduces punishment of up to five years in prison to people who blockade public buildings, and the arrest of protesters who wear masks or helmets. A large outcry, both domestic and international, leads to the repeal of the law on Jan. 27.

January 25

President Viktor Yanukovich offers the opposition the role of prime minister, which is quickly rejected. "This was a poisoned offer by Yanukovich to divide our protest movement. We will keep on negotiating and continue to demand early elections," says opposition leader Vitaly Klitschko, who is offered a deputy prime minister role.

January 30

A government bill offering protesters amnesty if they abandon occupied government buildings is met with contempt by the opposition. It's the latest of government concessions that the opposition says don't go far enough. Protesters demand President Viktor Yanukovich's resignation, early elections and the firing of authorities responsible for police violence.

February 16

In exchange for the release of all jailed protesters, anti-government demonstrators agree to leave Kiev's city hall, which they have been occupying since Dec. 1, 2013.

February 19

Following two days of violence that leaves up to 26 dead, President Viktor Yanukovich announces a truce with opposition leaders. The Ukrainian government and three main opposition leaders will start negotiations with the aim of ending bloodshed, and stabilizing the situation in the state in the interests of social peace.

February 20

Despite the truce announced on Feb. 19, Kiev's city health department says 67 people have been killed since the outbreak of violence on Feb. 18 – the worse violence to afflict the country since its independence. In response, the European Union announces sanctions on the country, including visa bans, asset freezes and restrictions on exporting anti-riot equipment. Just a day earlier on Feb. 19, the United States began sanctions by banning visas for 20 senior members of the Ukrainian government.

February 21

During talks brokered by EU ministers, President Yanukovich and opposition leaders sign a deal to hold presidential elections early, form a national unity government and make constitutional changes reducing his power. They agree that elections will be held as soon as a new constitution is adopted, no later than Dec. 2014. The agreement is met with widespread skepticism among protesters.

Ukraine's parliament votes to release former prime minister and opposition leader Yulia Tymoshenko from jail, where she had been held since 2011 on controversial charges of political corruption. A physical altercation erupts between ministers of parliament when the house speaker delays debate on a resolution to reduce President Yanukovich's powers.

February 22

Parliament votes to dismiss President Yanukovich, paving the way for presidential elections to be held on May 25. The vote came hours after opposition protestors overran his home and office in Kiev. Earlier in the day, Yanukovich insisted he would not step down. Ousting of the Ukraine President Viktor Yanukovych, and a push by pro-Russian protesters for Crimea to secede from Ukraine and seek assistance from Russia.

Fresh out of jail, former Prime Minister Yulia Tymoshenko acts quickly to secure opposition support — announcing plans to run for president and later, while addressing a crowd of tens of thousands of protesters in Kiev, urges them to remain in Independence Square, the epicenter of anti-government protest, until all their demands are met.

February 26

Thousands of pro-Russian and pro-Ukraine protesters clashed in front of the parliament building in Simferopol. On the same day Russian President Vladimir Putin put 2,000 Russian troops on alert along the Ukrainian border

February 27

The new Ukrainian ruling coalition — comprised of politicians and civilian activists — appoints former Economy Minister Arseny Yatsenyuk as prime minister, who will rule until presidential elections are held on May 25, 2014.

In the Crimea, where dismissed President Viktor Yanukovich fled before taking a ship to the safety of Russia, government buildings are taken over by armed men, as is the airport in the regional capital city of Simferopol.

February 28

Russian military forces occupied key posts, buildings, airports, and other assets in Crimea. The interim Government of Ukraine described the events as an invasion and occupation of Crimea. Crimean Prime Minister Sergey Aksyonov, elected in an emergency session earlier in the week, said he asserted sole control over Crimea's security forces and appealed to Russia for assistance in guaranteeing peace and calmness on the peninsula. The central Ukrainian government does not recognize the Aksyonov administration and considers it illegal. The Russian foreign ministry stated that *movement of the Black Sea Fleet armored vehicles in Crimea (...) happens in full accordance with basic Russian-Ukrainian agreements on the Black Sea Fleet.*

Armed men, described as local militia, storm two airports in the Crimean Peninsula, in both the Crimean capital of Simferopol and the major coastal port of Sevastopol. This comes a day after another group of men seized Crimea's regional parliament and replaced the Ukrainian flag with a Russian one.

March 1

The Russian parliament granted President Vladimir Putin the authority to use military force in Ukraine. The U.S. and the European Union condemned this move. On the same day, the acting president of Ukraine, Oleksandr Turchynov decreed the appointment of the Prime Minister of Crimea as unconstitutional.

March 6

The Crimean parliament voted in favour of joining Russia in a union between the two nations.

March 16

An official referendum on the matter was to be held on the 16th of March. However, the local referendum is not allowed according to the Ukrainian Constitution and laws, thus not legitimate.

March 24

Ukraine's acting president, Oleksandr Turchynov, said on television that all servicemen and their families would be relocated to the mainland. The national security and defence council has reached a decision, under instructions from the defence ministry, to conduct a redeployment of military units stationed in the Autonomous Republic of Crimea. The cabinet of ministers has instructions to resettle the families of soldiers as well as everyone else who today is forced to leave their homes under the pressure and aggression of the Russian army's occupying forces. Despite the enormous losses, the Ukrainian soldiers in Crimea did their duty. Most importantly, they gave the

Ukrainian armed forces the opportunity to prepare their defences, to put the military on full combat alert, and to launch a partial mobilisation.

Crimea's pro-Kremlin deputy premier, Rustam Temirgaliyev, had a slightly different take on it, saying:
All Ukrainian soldiers have either switched to the Russian side or are leaving the territory of the Crimea.

Russia says its flag is now flying over 189 military institutions in Crimea.

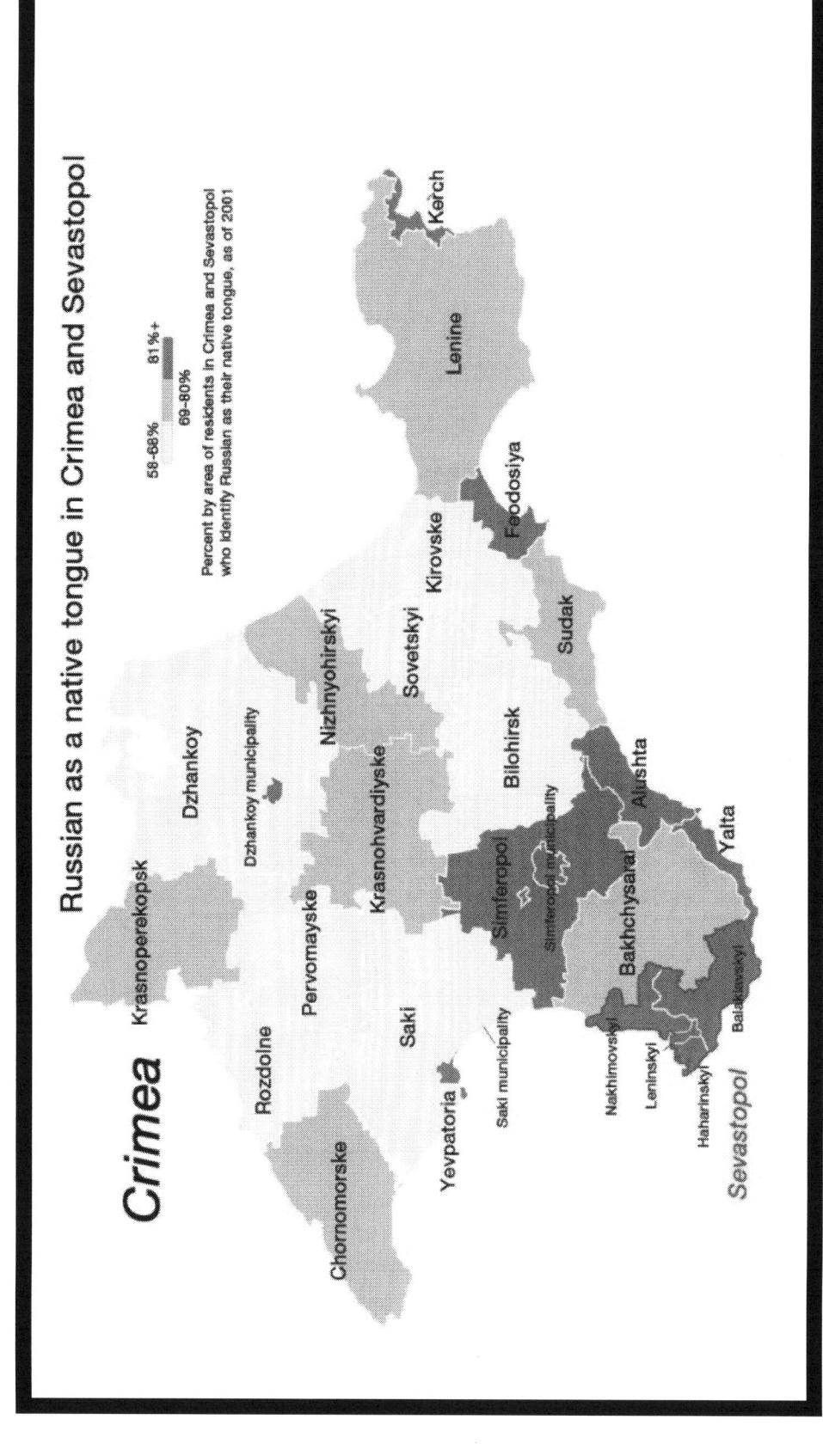

Printed in Great Britain
by Amazon